CW00495940

Top Essential

Air Fryer

Cookbook for Beginners

2000 Days of Super Easy, Yummy & Fast Air Fryer Recipes for Family Meals to Air Broil, Roast, Bake, Reheat, and Dehydrate | Every Age Love to Eat

Helen C. Harker

CONTENTS

INTRODUCTION

Hello, I'm Helen C. Harker, and I'm thrilled to introduce you to my Air Fryer Cookbook. I've spent most of my life in the world of culinary arts, with a passion for exploring new cooking techniques and creating delicious, wholesome meals. My journey started when I pursued a culinary degree at a renowned culinary institute, which ignited my love for experimenting with flavors and ingredients.

Throughout my career, I've worked as a professional chef in various restaurants and also had the privilege of teaching cooking classes to enthusiastic students eager to elevate their culinary skills. Over the years, I've witnessed the kitchen evolve with the introduction of innovative appliances, and one that has truly captured my attention is the air fryer.

The inspiration behind my Air Fryer Cookbook was to demystify this incredible kitchen gadget and make it accessible to everyone. I wanted to create a resource that not only provides a wide array of mouthwatering recipes but also offers step-by-step instructions, handy shopping lists, precise cooking times, and practical tips for successful air frying. Whether you're a seasoned home cook or just starting your culinary journey, this cookbook is designed to help you harness the power of the air fryer to prepare delectable dishes with ease.

So, whether you're looking to whip up quick weeknight dinners, prepare healthy snacks, or impress your friends and family with restaurant-quality appetizers, my Air Fryer Cookbook has something for you. Join me on this culinary adventure, and together, we'll explore the endless possibilities of cooking with the air fryer, creating meals that are not only delicious but also convenient and nutritious. Happy cooking!

GETTING TO KNOW AIR FRYER

An air fryer works by using rapidly circulating hot air to cook food. It has a heating element and a fan that blows the hot air around the food in a cooking chamber. The hot air quickly cooks the food and creates a crispy outer layer similar to frying, but with significantly less oil. The food is placed in a basket or on a tray, and as the hot air circulates, it cooks the food evenly and crisps it up. Air fryers are popular for their ability to produce crispy and delicious results while reducing the amount of oil needed, making them a healthier alternative to traditional deep frying.

COOKING MODE AND COMMON INGREDIENTS

For Whom	Common Cooking Modes	Common Ingredients	Recommended Temperatures (°F)	Tips and Notes
Busy Individuals	Air Fry, Reheat	Frozen Foods, Leftovers	350-400°F	Air fryers are great for quickly reheating and crisping up food.
Health-Conscious	Air Fry, Bake, Grill	Lean Meats, Vegetables	325-400°F	Use minimal oil for healthier options.
Vegetarians/Vegans	Air Fry, Roast	Tofu, Vegetables, Nuts	325-375°F	Toss ingredients with seasoning for flavor.
Families	Air Fry, Bake, Grill	Chicken, Potatoes, Fish	350-400°F	Cook larger batches with multiple trays.
Snack Lovers	Air Fry, Dehydrate	Chips, Fruit Slices, Jerky	125-200°F (Dehydrate)	Dehydrate fruits and make healthy snacks.
Cooking Enthusiasts	Air Fry, Roast, Broil	Steaks, Seafood, Pastries	Varied, depending on the dish	Experiment with various cooking modes for gourmet results.
Weight Watchers	Air Fry	Veggies, Poultry	350-375°F	Use the air fryer for low-calorie cooking.

THE BENEFITS OF AN AIR FRYER TO YOU

Reduced Oil Usage

Air fryers require significantly less oil than deep frying, which means you can enjoy crispy, fried-like textures with just a fraction of the fat and calories. In many cases, you can achieve a similar taste and texture with only a light coating of oil, or even without any oil at all, depending on the food you're cooking. This reduction in oil consumption is beneficial for heart health and weight management.

Lower Caloric Intake

Since air frying uses less oil, the calorie content of the cooked food is lower compared to deep-fried versions. This is particularly advantageous if you're looking to reduce your calorie intake or manage your weight while still enjoying fried foods.

Less Formation of Harmful Compounds

Deep frying at high temperatures can lead to the formation of potentially harmful compounds like acrylamides and trans fats, which are associated with health risks. Air frying, with its lower cooking temperatures and shorter cooking times, minimizes the formation of these compounds, making it a safer option.

Retains Nutrients

Air frying can help retain more of the nutrients present in food compared to deep frying. Since the cooking process is shorter and less harsh, vegetables, for example, can maintain a greater portion of their vitamins and minerals, contributing to a more nutritious meal.

Reduces Exposure to Hot Oil

Deep frying involves immersing food in hot oil, which can lead to splattering and burns if not done carefully. Air frying eliminates this risk, making it a safer cooking method, especially for those who may be concerned about accidents or are cooking with children.

REASONS FOR AIR FRYER COOKBOOK

1. **Maximizing Use of the Appliance:** Air fryers are versatile kitchen appliances, and a cookbook can help users make the most of their investment. Cookbooks provide a wide range of recipes and cooking techniques specifically tailored to air fryers.

2. **Convenience:** Air fryer cookbooks offer convenient and easy-to-follow recipes that simplify the cooking process. They often provide step-by-step instructions and cooking times, making it simpler for users, including beginners, to prepare meals.

3. **Healthy Cooking:** Many people turn to air fryers for healthier cooking options. Air fryer cookbooks often feature recipes that use less oil and produce crispy results without deep frying. This appeals to individuals who are health-conscious and looking to reduce their oil intake.

4. **Variety:** Cookbooks offer a variety of recipes, from appetizers to main courses and desserts, allowing users to diversify their meals. This is especially appealing to those who want to experiment with different cuisines and dishes.

5. **Inspiration:** Cookbooks can inspire creativity in the kitchen. They introduce new cooking methods and flavor combinations that users might not have thought of on their own. This can reignite a passion for cooking and trying out new recipes.

6. **Time-Saving:** Air fryers are known for their quick cooking times, and cookbooks often provide recipes that can be prepared in a fraction of the time it would take using conventional methods. This is a major draw for busy individuals and families.

BREAD AND BREAKFAST RECIPES

Thai Turkey Sausage Patties

Servings:4
Cooking Time: 30 Minutes

Ingredients:

- 12 oz turkey sausage
- 1 tsp onion powder
- 1 tsp dried coriander
- ¼ tsp Thai curry paste
- ¼ tsp red pepper flakes
- Salt and pepper to taste

Directions:

1. Preheat air fryer to 350°F. Place the sausage, onion, coriander, curry paste, red flakes, salt, and black pepper in a large bowl and mix well. Form into eight patties. Arrange the patties on the greased frying basket and Air Fry for 10 minutes, flipping once halfway through. Once the patties are cooked, transfer to a plate and serve hot.

Seafood Quinoa Frittata

Servings: 4
Cooking Time: 30 Minutes

Ingredients:

- ½ cup cooked shrimp, chopped
- ½ cup cooked quinoa
- ½ cup baby spinach
- 4 eggs
- ½ tsp dried basil
- 1 anchovy, chopped
- ½ cup grated cheddar

Directions:

1. Preheat air fryer to 320°F. Add quinoa, shrimp, and spinach to a greased baking pan. Set aside. Beat eggs, anchovy, and basil in a bowl until frothy. Pour over the quinoa mixture, then top with cheddar cheese. Bake until the frittata is puffed and golden, 14-18 minutes. Serve.

Spinach-bacon Rollups

Servings: 4
Cooking Time: 9 Minutes

Ingredients:

- 4 flour tortillas (6- or 7-inch size)
- 4 slices Swiss cheese
- 1 cup baby spinach leaves
- 4 slices turkey bacon

Directions:

1. Preheat air fryer to 390°F.
2. On each tortilla, place one slice of cheese and ¼ cup of spinach.
3. Roll up tortillas and wrap each with a strip of bacon. Secure each end with a toothpick.
4. Place rollups in air fryer basket, leaving a little space in between them.
5. Cook for 4minutes. Turn and rearrange rollups (for more even cooking) and cook for 5minutes longer, until bacon is crisp.

Blueberry French Toast Sticks

Servings: 4
Cooking Time: 20 Minutes

Ingredients:

- 3 bread slices, cut into strips
- 1 tbsp butter, melted
- 2 eggs
- 1 tbsp milk
- 1 tbsp sugar
- ½ tsp vanilla extract
- 1 cup fresh blueberries
- 1 tbsp lemon juice

Directions:

1. Preheat air fryer to 380°F. After laying the bread strips on a plate, sprinkle some melted butter over each piece. Whisk the eggs, milk, vanilla, and sugar, then dip the bread in the mix. Place on a wire rack to let the batter drip. Put the bread strips in the air fryer and Air Fry for 5-7 minutes. Use tongs to flip them once and cook until golden. With a fork, smash the blueberries and lemon juice together. Spoon the blueberries sauce over the French sticks. Serve immediately.

Morning Chicken Frittata Cups

Servings:6
Cooking Time: 30 Minutes

Ingredients:

- ¼ cup shredded cooked chicken breasts
- 3 eggs
- 2 tbsp heavy cream
- 4 tsp Tabasco sauce
- ¼ cup grated Asiago cheese
- 2 tbsp chives, chopped

Directions:

1. Preheat air fryer to 350ºF. Beat all ingredients in a bowl. Divide the egg mixture between greased 6 muffin cups and place them in the frying basket. Bake for 8-10 minutes until set. Let cool slightly before serving. Enjoy!

Pesto Egg & Ham Sandwiches

Servings: 2
Cooking Time: 20 Minutes

Ingredients:

- 4 sandwich bread slices
- 2 tbsp butter, melted
- 4 eggs, scrambled
- 4 deli ham slices
- 2 Colby cheese slices
- 4 tsp basil pesto sauce
- ¼ tsp red chili flakes
- ¼ sliced avocado

Directions:

1. Preheat air fryer at 370ºF. Brush 2 pieces of bread with half of the butter and place them, butter side down, into the frying basket. Divide eggs, chili flakes, sliced avocado, ham, and cheese on each bread slice.
2. Spread pesto on the remaining bread slices and place them, pesto side-down, onto the sandwiches. Brush the remaining butter on the tops of the sandwiches and Bake for 6 minutes, flipping once. Serve immediately.

Smoked Salmon Croissant Sandwich

Servings: 1
Cooking Time: 30 Minutes

Ingredients:

- 1 croissant, halved
- 2 eggs
- 1 tbsp guacamole
- 1 smoked salmon slice
- Salt and pepper to taste

Directions:

1. Preheat air fryer to 360°F. Place the croissant, crusty side up, in the frying basket side by side. Whisk the eggs in a small ceramic dish until fluffy. Place in the air fryer. Bake for 10 minutes. Gently scramble the half-cooked egg in the baking dish with a fork. Flip the croissant and cook for another 10 minutes until the scrambled eggs are cooked, but still fluffy, and the croissant is toasted.
2. Place one croissant on a serving plate, then spread the guacamole on top. Scoop the scrambled eggs onto guacamole, then top with smoked salmon. Sprinkle with salt and pepper. Top with the second slice of toasted croissant, close sandwich, and serve hot.

Bagels With Avocado & Tomatoes

Servings: 2
Cooking Time: 35 Minutes

Ingredients:

- 2/3 cup all-purpose flour
- ½ tsp active dry yeast
- 1/3 cup Greek yogurt
- 8 cherry tomatoes
- 1 ripe avocado
- 1 tbsp lemon juice
- 2 tbsp chopped red onions
- Black pepper to taste

Directions:

1. Preheat air fryer to 400°F. Beat the flour, dry yeast, and Greek yogurt until you get a smooth dough, adding more flour if necessary. Make 2 equal balls out of the mixture.
2. Using a rolling pin, roll each ball into a 9-inch long strip. Form a ring with each strip and press the ends together to create 2 bagels. In a bowl with hot water, soak the bagels for 1 minute. Shake excess water and let rise for 15 minutes in the fryer. Bake for 5 minutes, turn the bagels, top with tomatoes, and Bake for another 5 minutes.
3. Cut avocado in half, discard the pit and remove the flesh into a bowl. Mash with a fork and stir in lemon juice and onions. Once the bagels are ready, let cool slightly and cut them in half. Spread on each half some guacamole, top with 2 slices of Baked tomatoes, and sprinkle with pepper. Serve immediately.

Cinnamon Pumpkin Donuts

Servings: 6
Cooking Time: 30 Minutes

Ingredients:

- 1/3 cup canned pumpkin purée
- 1 cup flour
- 3 tbsp brown sugar
- ½ tsp ground cinnamon
- 1/8 tsp ground nutmeg
- 1 tsp baking powder
- 3 tbsp milk
- 2 tbsp butter, melted
- 1 large egg
- 3 tbsp powdered sugar

Directions:

1. Combine the flour, brown sugar, cinnamon, nutmeg, and baking powder in a bowl. Whisk the pumpkin, milk, butter, and egg white in another bowl. Pour the pumpkin mixture over the dry ingredients and stir. Add more milk or flour if necessary to make a soft dough.Cover your hands in flour, make 12 pieces from the dough, and form them into balls. Measure the frying basket, then cut foil or parchment paper about an inch smaller than the measurement. Poke holes in it and put it in the basket.
2. Preheat air fryer to 360°F. Set the donut holes in the basket and Air Fry for 5-7 minutes. Allow the donuts to chill for 5 minutes, then roll in powdered sugar. Serve.

Meaty Omelet

Servings: 4
Cooking Time: 20 Minutes

Ingredients:

- 6 eggs
- ½ cup grated Swiss cheese
- 3 breakfast sausages, sliced
- 8 bacon strips, sliced
- Salt and pepper to taste

Directions:

1. Preheat air fryer to 360°F. In a bowl, beat the eggs and stir in Swiss cheese, sausages and bacon. Transfer the mixture to a baking dish and set in the fryer. Bake for 15 minutes or until golden and crisp. Season and serve.

Quiche Cups

Servings: 10
Cooking Time: 16 Minutes

Ingredients:

- ¼ pound all-natural ground pork sausage
- 3 eggs
- ¾ cup milk
- 20 foil muffin cups
- cooking spray
- 4 ounces sharp Cheddar cheese, grated

Directions:

1. Divide sausage into 3 portions and shape each into a thin patty.
2. Place patties in air fryer basket and cook 390°F for 6minutes.
3. While sausage is cooking, prepare the egg mixture. A large measuring cup or bowl with a pouring lip works best. Combine the eggs and milk and whisk until well blended. Set aside.
4. When sausage has cooked fully, remove patties from basket, drain well, and use a fork to crumble the meat into small pieces.
5. Double the foil cups into 10 sets. Remove paper liners from the top muffin cups and spray the foil cups lightly with cooking spray.
6. Divide crumbled sausage among the 10 muffin cup sets.
7. Top each with grated cheese, divided evenly among the cups.
8. Place 5 cups in air fryer basket.
9. Pour egg mixture into each cup, filling until each cup is at least ⅔ full.
10. Cook for 8 minutes and test for doneness. A knife inserted into the center shouldn't have any raw egg on it when removed.
11. If needed, cook 2 more minutes, until egg completely sets.
12. Repeat steps 8 through 11 for the remaining quiches.

Mini Bacon Egg Quiches

Servings:6
Cooking Time: 30 Minutes

Ingredients:

- 3 eggs
- 2 tbsp heavy cream
- ¼ tsp Dijon mustard
- Salt and pepper to taste
- 3 oz cooked bacon, crumbled
- ¼ cup grated cheddar

Directions:

1. Preheat air fryer to 350ºF. Beat the eggs with salt and pepper in a bowl until fluffy. Stir in heavy cream, mustard, cooked bacon, and cheese. Divide the mixture between 6 greased muffin cups and place them in the frying basket. Bake for 8-10 minutes. Let cool slightly before serving.

Chocolate Almond Crescent Rolls

Servings: 4
Cooking Time: 8 Minutes

Ingredients:

- 1 (8-ounce) tube of crescent roll dough
- ⅔ cup semi-sweet or bittersweet chocolate chunks
- 1 egg white, lightly beaten
- ¼ cup sliced almonds
- powdered sugar, for dusting
- butter or oil

Directions:

1. Preheat the air fryer to 350°F.
2. Unwrap the crescent roll dough and separate it into triangles with the points facing away from you. Place a row of chocolate chunks along the bottom edge of the dough. (If you are using chips, make it a double row.) Roll the dough up around the chocolate and then place another row of chunks on the dough. Roll again and finish with one or two chocolate chunks. Be sure to leave the end free of chocolate so that it can adhere to the rest of the roll.
3. Brush the tops of the crescent rolls with the lightly beaten egg white and sprinkle the almonds on top, pressing them into the crescent dough so they adhere.
4. Brush the bottom of the air fryer basket with butter or oil and transfer the crescent rolls to the basket. Air-fry at 350°F for 8 minutes. Remove and let the crescent rolls cool before dusting with powdered sugar and serving.

Parsley Egg Scramble With Cottage Cheese

Servings:2
Cooking Time: 15 Minutes

Ingredients:

- 1 tbsp cottage cheese, crumbled
- 4 eggs
- Salt and pepper to taste
- 2 tsp heavy cream
- 1 tbsp chopped parsley

Directions:

1. Preheat air fryer to 400ºF. Grease a baking pan with olive oil. Beat the eggs, salt, and pepper in a bowl. Pour it into the pan, place the pan in the frying basket, and Air Fry for 5 minutes. Using a silicone spatula, stir in heavy cream, cottage cheese, and half of parsley and Air Fry for another 2 minutes. Scatter with parsley to serve.

Sweet Potato-cinnamon Toast

Servings: 6
Cooking Time: 8 Minutes

Ingredients:

- 1 small sweet potato, cut into ⅜-inch slices
- oil for misting
- ground cinnamon

Directions:

1. Preheat air fryer to 390°F.
2. Spray both sides of sweet potato slices with oil. Sprinkle both sides with cinnamon to taste.
3. Place potato slices in air fryer basket in a single layer.
4. Cook for 4minutes, turn, and cook for 4 more minutes or until potato slices are barely fork tender.

Country Gravy

Servings: 2
Cooking Time: 7 Minutes

Ingredients:

- ¼ pound pork sausage, casings removed
- 1 tablespoon butter
- 2 tablespoons flour
- 2 cups whole milk
- ½ teaspoon salt
- freshly ground black pepper
- 1 teaspoon fresh thyme leaves

Directions:

1. Preheat a saucepan over medium heat. Add and brown the sausage, crumbling it into small pieces as it cooks. Add the butter and flour, stirring well to combine. Continue to cook for 2 minutes, stirring constantly.
2. Slowly pour in the milk, whisking as you do, and bring the mixture to a boil to thicken. Season with salt and freshly ground black pepper, lower the heat and simmer until the sauce has thickened to your desired consistency – about 5 minutes. Stir in the fresh thyme, season to taste and serve hot.

Avocado Toasts With Poached Eggs

Servings: 4
Cooking Time: 15 Minutes

Ingredients:

- 4 eggs
- Salt and pepper to taste
- 4 bread pieces, toasted
- 1 pitted avocado, sliced
- ½ tsp chili powder
- ½ tsp dried rosemary

Directions:

1. Preheat air fryer to 320°F. Crack 1 egg into each greased ramekin and season with salt and black pepper. Place the ramekins into the air frying basket. Bake for 6-8 minutes.
2. Scoop the flesh of the avocado into a small bowl. Season with salt, black pepper, chili powderp and rosemary. Using a fork, smash the avocado lightly. Spread the smashed avocado evenly over toasted bread slices. Remove the eggs from the air fryer and gently spoon one onto each slice of avocado toast. Serve and enjoy!

Western Frittata

Servings: 1
Cooking Time: 19 Minutes

Ingredients:

- ½ red or green bell pepper, cut into ½-inch chunks
- 1 teaspoon olive oil
- 3 eggs, beaten
- ¼ cup grated Cheddar cheese
- ¼ cup diced cooked ham
- salt and freshly ground black pepper, to taste
- 1 teaspoon butter
- 1 teaspoon chopped fresh parsley

Directions:

1. Preheat the air fryer to 400°F.
2. Toss the peppers with the olive oil and air-fry for 6 minutes, shaking the basket once or twice during the cooking process to redistribute the ingredients.
3. While the vegetables are cooking, beat the eggs well in a bowl, stir in the Cheddar cheese and ham, and season with salt and freshly ground black pepper. Add the air-fried peppers to this bowl when they have finished cooking.
4. Place a 6- or 7-inch non-stick metal cake pan into the air fryer basket with the butter using an aluminum sling to lower the pan into the basket. (Fold a piece of aluminum foil into a strip about 2-inches wide by 24-inches long.) Air-fry for 1 minute at 380°F to melt the butter. Remove the cake pan and rotate the pan to distribute the butter and grease the pan. Pour the egg mixture into the cake pan and return the pan to the air fryer, using the aluminum sling.
5. Air-fry at 380°F for 12 minutes, or until the frittata has puffed up and is lightly browned. Let the frittata sit in the air fryer for 5 minutes to cool to an edible temperature and set up. Remove the cake pan from the air fryer, sprinkle with parsley and serve immediately.

APPETIZERS AND SNACKS RECIPES

Balsamic Grape Dip

Servings: 6
Cooking Time: 25 Minutes

Ingredients:

- 2 cups seedless red grapes
- 1 tbsp balsamic vinegar
- 1 tbsp honey
- 1 cup Greek yogurt
- 2 tbsp milk
- 2 tbsp minced fresh basil

Directions:

1. Preheat air fryer to 380°F. Add the grapes and balsamic vinegar to the frying basket, then pour honey over and toss to coat. Roast for 8-12 minutes, shriveling the grapes, and take them out of the air fryer. Mix the milk and yogurt together, then gently stir in the grapes and basil. Serve and enjoy!

Bacon-wrapped Goat Cheese Poppers

Servings: 10
Cooking Time: 10 Minutes

Ingredients:

- 10 large jalapeño peppers
- 8 ounces goat cheese
- 10 slices bacon

Directions:

1. Preheat the air fryer to 380°F.
2. Slice the jalapeños in half. Carefully remove the veins and seeds of the jalapeños with a spoon.
3. Fill each jalapeño half with 2 teaspoons goat cheese.
4. Cut the bacon in half lengthwise to make long strips. Wrap the jalapeños with bacon, trying to cover the entire length of the jalapeño.
5. Place the bacon-wrapped jalapeños into the air fryer basket. Cook the stuffed jalapeños for 10 minutes or until bacon is crispy.

Nicoise Deviled Eggs

Servings:4
Cooking Time: 20 Minutes

Ingredients:

- 4 eggs
- 2 tbsp mayonnaise
- 10 chopped Nicoise olives
- 2 tbsp goat cheese crumbles
- Salt and pepper to taste
- 2 tbsp chopped parsley

Directions:

1. Preheat air fryer to 260°F. Place the eggs in silicone muffin cups to avoid bumping around and cracking during the cooking process. Add silicone cups to the frying basket and Air Fry for 15 minutes. Remove and run the eggs under cold water. When cool, remove the shells and halve them lengthwise.
2. Spoon yolks into a separate medium bowl and arrange white halves on a large plate. Mash the yolks with a fork. Stir in the remaining ingredients. Spoon mixture into white halves and scatter with mint to serve.

Crispy Tofu Bites

Servings: 4
Cooking Time: 20 Minutes

Ingredients:

- 1 pound Extra firm unflavored tofu
- Vegetable oil spray

Directions:

1. Wrap the piece of tofu in a triple layer of paper towels. Place it on a wooden cutting board and set a large pot on top of it to press out excess moisture. Set aside for 10 minutes.
2. Preheat the air fryer to 400°F.
3. Remove the pot and unwrap the tofu. Cut it into 1-inch cubes. Place these in a bowl and coat them generously with vegetable oil spray. Toss gently, then spray generously again before tossing, until all are glistening.
4. Gently pour the tofu pieces into the basket, spread them into as close to one layer as possible, and air-fry for 20 minutes, using kitchen tongs to gently rearrange the pieces at the 7- and 14-minute marks, until light brown and crisp.
5. Gently pour the tofu pieces onto a wire rack. Cool for 5 minutes before serving warm.

Sweet Chili Peanuts

Servings: 6
Cooking Time: 5 Minutes

Ingredients:

- 2 cups (10 ounces) Shelled raw peanuts
- 2 tablespoons Granulated white sugar
- 2 teaspoons Hot red pepper sauce, such as Cholula or Tabasco (gluten-free, if a concern)

Directions:

1. Preheat the air fryer to 400°F.
2. Toss the peanuts, sugar, and hot pepper sauce in a bowl until the peanuts are well coated.
3. When the machine is at temperature, pour the peanuts into the basket, spreading them into one layer as much as you can. Air-fry undisturbed for 3 minutes.
4. Shake the basket to rearrange the peanuts. Continue air-frying for 2 minutes more, shaking and stirring the peanuts every 30 seconds, until golden brown.
5. Pour the peanuts onto a large lipped baking sheet. Spread them into one layer and cool for 5 minutes before serving.

Fried Gyoza

Servings: 18
Cooking Time: 6 Minutes

Ingredients:

- 5 ounces Lean ground pork
- 2½ tablespoons Very thinly sliced scallion
- 1 tablespoon plus 2 teaspoons Minced peeled fresh ginger
- 1¼ teaspoons Toasted sesame oil
- ⅛ teaspoon Table salt
- ⅛ teaspoon Ground black pepper
- 18 Round gyoza or square wonton wrappers (thawed, if necessary)
- Vegetable oil spray

Directions:

1. Preheat the air fryer to 350°F .
2. Mix the ground pork, scallion, ginger, sesame oil, salt, and pepper in a bowl until well combined.
3. Set a bowl of water on a clean, dry surface or next to a clean, dry cutting board. Set one gyoza or wonton wrapper on that surface. Dip your clean finger in the water and run it around the perimeter of the gyoza wrapper or the edge of the wonton wrapper. Put about 1 ½ teaspoons of the meat mixture in the center of the wrapper.
4. For the gyoza wrapper, fold the wrapper in half to close, pressing the edge to seal, then wet the outside of the edge of both sides of the seam and pleat it into little ridges to seal.
5. For the wonton wrapper, fold it in half lengthwise to make a rectangle, then seal the sides together, flattening the packet a bit as you do.
6. Set the filled wrapper aside and continue making more in the same way. When done, generously coat them on all sides with vegetable oil spray.
7. Place the gyoza in the basket in one layer and air-fry undisturbed for 6 minutes, or until browned and crisp at the edges.
8. Use kitchen tongs or a nonstick-safe spatula to gently transfer the gyoza to a wire rack. Cool for only 2 or 3 minutes before serving hot.

Poutine

Servings: 2
Cooking Time: 25 Minutes

Ingredients:

- 2 russet potatoes, scrubbed and cut into ½-inch sticks
- 2 teaspoons vegetable oil
- 2 tablespoons butter
- ¼ onion, minced (about ¼ cup)
- 1 clove garlic, smashed
- ¼ teaspoon dried thyme
- 3 tablespoons flour
- 1 teaspoon tomato paste
- 1½ cups strong beef stock
- salt and lots of freshly ground black pepper
- a few dashes of Worcestershire sauce
- ⅔ cup chopped string cheese or cheese curds

Directions:

1. Bring a large saucepan of salted water to a boil on the stovetop while you peel and cut the potatoes. Blanch the potatoes in the boiling salted water for 4 minutes while you Preheat the air fryer to 400°F. Strain the potatoes and rinse them with cold water. Dry them well with a clean kitchen towel.
2. Toss the dried potato sticks gently with the oil and place them in the air fryer basket. Air-fry for 25 minutes, shaking the basket a few times while the fries cook to help them brown evenly.
3. While the fries are cooking, make the gravy. Melt the butter in a small saucepan over medium heat. Add the onion, garlic and thyme and cook for five minutes, until soft and just starting to brown. Stir in the flour and cook for another two minutes, stirring regularly. Finally, add the tomato paste and continue to cook for another minute or two. Whisk in the beef stock and bring the mixture to a boil to thicken. Season to taste with salt, lots of freshly ground black pepper and a few dashes of Worcestershire sauce. Keep the gravy warm.
4. As soon as the fries are done, season them with salt and transfer to a plate or basket. Top the fries with the cheese curds or string cheese, and pour the warm gravy over the top.

Crispy Spiced Chickpeas

Servings: 2
Cooking Time: 20 Minutes

Ingredients:

- 1 (15-ounce) can chickpeas, drained (or 1½ cups cooked chickpeas)
- ½ teaspoon salt
- ½ teaspoon chili powder
- ¼ teaspoon ground cinnamon
- ⅛ teaspoon smoked paprika
- pinch ground cayenne pepper
- 1 tablespoon olive oil

Directions:

1. Preheat the air fryer to 400°F.
2. Dry the chickpeas as well as you can with a clean kitchen towel, rubbing off any loose skins as necessary. Combine the spices in a small bowl. Toss the chickpeas with the olive oil and then add the spices and toss again.
3. Air-fry for 15 minutes, shaking the basket a couple of times while they cook.
4. Check the chickpeas to see if they are crispy enough and if necessary, air-fry for another 5 minutes to crisp them further. Serve warm, or cool to room temperature and store in an airtight container for up to two weeks.

Orange-glazed Carrots

Servings: 3
Cooking Time: 25 Minutes

Ingredients:

- 3 carrots, cut into spears
- 1 tbsp orange juice
- 2 tsp balsamic vinegar
- 1 tsp avocado oil
- 1 tsp clear honey
- ½ tsp dried rosemary
- ¼ tsp salt
- ¼ tsp lemon zest

Directions:

1. Preheat air fryer to 390°F. Put the carrots in a baking pan. Add the orange juice, balsamic vinegar, oil, honey, rosemary, salt, and zest. Stir well. Roast for 15-18 minutes, shaking them once or twice until the carrots are bright orange, glazed, and tender. Serve while hot.

Prosciutto Mozzarella Bites

Servings: 8
Cooking Time: 6 Minutes

Ingredients:

- 8 pieces full-fat mozzarella string cheese
- 8 thin slices prosciutto
- 16 basil leaves

Directions:

1. Preheat the air fryer to 360°F.
2. Cut the string cheese in half across the center, not lengthwise. Do the same with the prosciutto.
3. Place a piece of prosciutto onto a clean workspace. Top the prosciutto with a basil leaf and then a piece of string cheese. Roll up the string cheese inside the prosciutto and secure with a wooden toothpick. Repeat with the remaining cheese sticks.
4. Place the prosciutto mozzarella bites into the air fryer basket and cook for 6 minutes, checking for doneness at 4 minutes.

Tomato & Halloumi Bruschetta

Servings: 4
Cooking Time: 20 Minutes

Ingredients:

- 2 tbsp softened butter
- 8 French bread slices
- 1 cup grated halloumi cheese
- ½ cup basil pesto
- 12 chopped cherry tomatoes
- 2 green onions, thinly sliced

Directions:

1. Preheat air fryer to 350°F. Spread butter on one side of the bread. Place butter-side up in the frying basket. Bake until the bread is slightly brown, 3-5 minutes. Remove the bread and top it with halloumi cheese. Melt the cheese on the bread in the air fryer for another 1-3 minutes.
2. Meanwhile, mix pesto, cherry tomatoes, and green onions in a small bowl. When the cheese has melted, take the bread out of the fryer and arrange on a plate. Top with pesto mix and serve.

Beer Battered Onion Rings

Servings: 2
Cooking Time: 16 Minutes

Ingredients:

- ⅔ cup flour
- ½ teaspoon baking soda
- 1 teaspoon paprika
- 1 teaspoon salt
- ½ teaspoon freshly ground black pepper
- ¾ cup beer
- 1 egg, beaten
- 1½ cups fine breadcrumbs
- 1 large Vidalia onion, peeled and sliced into ½-inch rings
- vegetable oil

Directions:

1. Set up a dredging station. Mix the flour, baking soda, paprika, salt and pepper together in a bowl. Pour in the beer, add the egg and whisk until smooth. Place the breadcrumbs in a cake pan or shallow dish.
2. Separate the onion slices into individual rings. Dip each onion ring into the batter with a fork. Lift the onion ring out of the batter and let any excess batter drip off. Then place the onion ring in the breadcrumbs and shake the cake pan back and forth to coat the battered onion ring. Pat the ring gently with your hands to make sure the breadcrumbs stick and that both sides of the ring are covered. Place the coated onion ring on a sheet pan and repeat with the rest of the onion rings.
3. Preheat the air fryer to 360°F.
4. Lightly spray the onion rings with oil, coating both sides. Layer the onion rings in the air fryer basket, stacking them on top of each other in a haphazard manner.
5. Air-fry for 10 minutes at 360°F. Flip the onion rings over and rotate the onion rings from the bottom of the basket to the top. Air-fry for an additional 6 minutes.
6. Serve immediately with your favorite dipping sauce.

Greek Street Tacos

Servings: 8
Cooking Time: 3 Minutes

Ingredients:

- 8 small flour tortillas (4-inch diameter)
- 8 tablespoons hummus
- 4 tablespoons crumbled feta cheese
- 4 tablespoons chopped kalamata or other olives (optional)
- olive oil for misting

Directions:

1. Place 1 tablespoon of hummus or tapenade in the center of each tortilla. Top with 1 teaspoon of feta crumbles and 1 teaspoon of chopped olives, if using.
2. Using your finger or a small spoon, moisten the edges of the tortilla all around with water.
3. Fold tortilla over to make a half-moon shape. Press center gently. Then press the edges firmly to seal in the filling.
4. Mist both sides with olive oil.
5. Place in air fryer basket very close but try not to overlap.
6. Cook at 390°F for 3minutes, just until lightly browned and crispy.

Home-style Buffalo Chicken Wings

Servings: 4
Cooking Time: 35 Minutes

Ingredients:

- 2 lb chicken wing portions
- 6 tbsp chili sauce
- 1 tsp dried oregano
- 1 tsp smoked paprika
- 1tsp garlic powder
- ½ tsp salt
- ¼ cup crumbled blue cheese
- 1/3 cup low-fat yogurt
- ½ tbsp lemon juice
- ½ tbsp white wine vinegar
- 2 celery stalks, cut into sticks
- 2 carrots, cut into sticks

Directions:

1. Add chicken with 1 tbsp of chili sauce, oregano, garlic, paprika, and salt to a large bowl. Toss to coat well, then set aside. In a small bowl, mash blue cheese and yogurt with a fork. Stir lemon juice and vinegar until smooth and blended. Refrigerate covered until it is time to serve.
2. Preheat air fryer to 300°F. Place the chicken in the greased frying basket and Air Fry for 22 minutes, flipping the chicken once until crispy and browned. Set aside in a clean bowl. Coat with the remaining tbsp of chili sauce. Serve with celery, carrot sticks and the blue cheese dip.

Cheesy Potato Canapés With Bacon

Servings: 4
Cooking Time: 35 Minutes

Ingredients:

- 4 bacon slices
- 4 russet potatoes, sliced
- 1 tbsp olive oil
- 1 tsp mustard powder
- Salt and pepper to taste
- 1 cup grated cheddar
- 2 tsp chopped chives
- 2 tsp chopped scallions

Directions:

1. Cook bacon in a skillet for 5 minutes over medium heat. Drain on a paper towel and crumble. Set aside. Add the potatoes to a large bowl and coat them with olive oil, mustard powder, salt and pepper.
2. Preheat air fryer to 400°F. Place the potatoes in the greased frying basket. Air Fry for 10 minutes. Shake the basket and cook for another 5-8 minutes or until potatoes are cooked through and edges are crisp. Transfer the potato bites to a serving dish. Serve warm topped with cheese, bacon, chives, and scallions.

Crunchy Tortellini Bites

Servings: 5
Cooking Time: 10 Minutes

Ingredients:

- 10 ounces (about 2½ cups) Cheese tortellini
- ⅓ cup Yellow cornmeal
- ⅓ cup Seasoned Italian-style dried bread crumbs
- ⅓ cup (about 1 ounce) Finely grated Parmesan cheese
- 1 Large egg
- Olive oil spray

Directions:

1. Bring a large pot of water to a boil over high heat. Add the tortellini and cook for 3 minutes. Drain in a colander set in the sink, then spread out the tortellini on a large baking sheet and cool for 15 minutes.
2. Preheat the air fryer to 400°F.
3. Mix the cornmeal, bread crumbs, and cheese in a large zip-closed plastic bag.
4. Whisk the egg in a medium bowl until uniform. Add the tortellini and toss well to coat, even along the inside curve of the pasta. Use a slotted spoon or kitchen tongs to transfer 5 or 6 tortellini to the plastic bag, seal, and shake gently to coat thoroughly and evenly. Set the coated tortellini aside on a cutting board and continue coating the rest in the same way.
5. Generously coat the tortellini on all sides with the olive oil spray, then set them in one layer in the basket. Air-fry undisturbed for 10 minutes, gently tossing the basket and rearranging the tortellini at the 4- and 7-minute marks, until brown and crisp.
6. Pour the contents of the basket onto a wire rack. Cool for 5 minutes before serving.

Fried String Beans With Greek Sauce

Servings: 4
Cooking Time: 10 Minutes

Ingredients:

- 1 egg
- 1 tbsp flour
- ¼ tsp paprika
- ½ tsp garlic powder
- Salt to taste
- ¼ cup bread crumbs
- ¼ lemon zest
- ½ lb whole string beans
- ½ cup Greek yogurt
- 1 tbsp lemon juice
- ⅛ tsp cayenne pepper

Directions:

1. Preheat air fryer to 380°F. Whisk the egg and 2 tbsp of water in a bowl until frothy. Sift the flour, paprika, garlic powder, and salt in another bowl, then stir in the bread crumbs. Dip each string bean into the egg mixture, then roll into the bread crumb mixture. Put the string beans in a single layer in the greased frying basket. Air Fry them for 5 minutes until the breading is golden brown. Stir the yogurt, lemon juice and zest, salt, and cayenne in a small bowl. Serve the bean fries with lemon-yogurt sauce.

Vegetarian Fritters With Green Dip

Servings: 6
Cooking Time: 40 Minutes

Ingredients:

- ½ cup grated carrots
- ½ cup grated zucchini
- ¼ cup minced yellow onion
- 1 garlic clove, minced
- 1 large egg
- ¼ cup flour
- ¼ cup bread crumbs
- Salt and pepper to taste
- ½ tsp ground cumin
- ½ avocado, peeled and pitted
- ½ cup plain Greek yogurt
- 1 tsp lime juice
- 1 tbsp white vinegar
- ¼ cup chopped cilantro

Directions:

1. Preheat air fryer to 375°F. Combine carrots, zucchini, onion, garlic, egg, flour, bread crumbs, salt, pepper, and cumin in a large bowl. Scoop out 12 equal portions of the vegetables and form them into patties. Arrange the patties on the greased basket. Air Fry for 5 minutes, then flip the patties. Air Fry for another 5 minutes. Check if the fritters are golden and cooked through. If more time is needed, cook for another 3-5 minutes.
2. While the fritters are cooking, prepare the avocado sauce. Mash the avocado in a small bowl to the desired texture. Stir in yogurt, white vinegar, chopped cilantro, lime juice, and salt. When the fritter is done, transfer to a serving plate along with the avocado sauce for dipping. Serve warm and enjoy.

VEGETABLE SIDE DISHES RECIPES

Fried Cauliflowerwith Parmesan Lemon Dressing

Servings: 2
Cooking Time: 12 Minutes

Ingredients:

- 4 cups cauliflower florets (about half a large head)
- 1 tablespoon olive oil
- salt and freshly ground black pepper
- 1 teaspoon finely chopped lemon zest
- 1 tablespoon fresh lemon juice (about half a lemon)
- ¼ cup grated Parmigiano-Reggiano cheese
- 4 tablespoons extra virgin olive oil
- ¼ teaspoon salt
- lots of freshly ground black pepper
- 1 tablespoon chopped fresh parsley

Directions:

1. Preheat the air fryer to 400°F.
2. Toss the cauliflower florets with the olive oil, salt and freshly ground black pepper. Air-fry for 12 minutes, shaking the basket a couple of times during the cooking process.
3. While the cauliflower is frying, make the dressing. Combine the lemon zest, lemon juice, Parmigiano-Reggiano cheese and olive oil in a small bowl. Season with salt and lots of freshly ground black pepper. Stir in the parsley.
4. Turn the fried cauliflower out onto a serving platter and drizzle the dressing over the top.

Beet Fries

Servings: 3
Cooking Time: 22 Minutes

Ingredients:

- 3 6-ounce red beets
- Vegetable oil spray
- To taste Coarse sea salt or kosher salt

Directions:

1. Preheat the air fryer to 375°F .
2. Remove the stems from the beets and peel them with a knife or vegetable peeler. Slice them into ½-inch-thick circles. Lay these flat on a cutting board and slice them into ½-inch-thick sticks. Generously coat the sticks on all sides with vegetable oil spray.
3. When the machine is at temperature, drop them into the basket, shake the basket to even the sticks out into as close to one layer as possible, and air-fry for 20 minutes, tossing and rearranging the beet matchsticks every 5 minutes, or until brown and even crisp at the ends. If the machine is at 360°F, you may need to add 2 minutes to the cooking time.
4. Pour the fries into a big bowl, add the salt, toss well, and serve warm.

Garlicky Brussels Sprouts

Servings: 4
Cooking Time: 35 Minutes

Ingredients:

- 1 lb Brussels sprouts, halved lengthwise
- 1 tbsp olive oil
- 1 tbsp lemon juice
- ½ tsp sea salt
- ⅛ tsp garlic powder
- 4 garlic cloves, sliced
- 2 tbsp parsley, chopped
- ½ tsp red chili flakes

Directions:

1. Preheat the air fryer to 375°F. Combine the olive oil, lemon juice, salt, and garlic powder in a bowl and mix well. Add the Brussels sprouts and toss to coat. Put the Brussels sprouts in the frying basket. Air Fry for 15-20 minutes, shaking the basket once until golden and crisp. Sprinkle with garlic slices, parsley, and chili flakes. Toss and cook for 2-4 minutes more until the garlic browns a bit.

Asparagus

Servings: 4
Cooking Time: 9 Minutes

Ingredients:

- 1 bunch asparagus (approx. 1 pound), washed and trimmed
- ⅛ teaspoon dried tarragon, crushed
- salt and pepper
- 1 to 2 teaspoons extra-light olive oil

Directions:

1. Spread asparagus spears on cookie sheet or cutting board.
2. Sprinkle with tarragon, salt, and pepper.
3. Drizzle with 1 teaspoon of oil and roll the spears or mix by hand. If needed, add up to 1 more teaspoon of oil and mix again until all spears are lightly coated.
4. Place spears in air fryer basket. If necessary, bend the longer spears to make them fit. It doesn't matter if they don't lie flat.
5. Cook at 390°F for 5minutes. Shake basket or stir spears with a spoon.
6. Cook for an additional 4 minutes or just until crisp-tender.

Charred Radicchio Salad

Servings: 4
Cooking Time: 5 Minutes

Ingredients:

- 2 Small 5- to 6-ounce radicchio head(s)
- 3 tablespoons Olive oil
- ½ teaspoon Table salt
- 2 tablespoons Balsamic vinegar
- Up to ¼ teaspoon Red pepper flakes

Directions:

1. Preheat the air fryer to 375°F .
2. Cut the radicchio head(s) into quarters through the stem end. Brush the oil over the heads, particularly getting it between the leaves along the cut sides. Sprinkle the radicchio quarters with the salt.
3. When the machine is at temperature, set the quarters cut sides up in the basket with as much air space between them as possible. They should not touch. Air-fry undisturbed for 5 minutes, watching carefully because they burn quickly, until blackened in bits and soft.
4. Use a nonstick-safe spatula to transfer the quarters to a cutting board. Cool for a minute or two, then cut out the thick stems inside the heads. Discard these tough bits and chop the remaining heads into bite-size bits. Scrape them into a bowl. Add the vinegar and red pepper flakes. Toss well and serve warm.

Street Corn

Servings: 4
Cooking Time: 10 Minutes

Ingredients:

- 1 tablespoon butter
- 4 ears corn
- ⅓ cup plain Greek yogurt
- 2 tablespoons Parmesan cheese
- ½ teaspoon paprika
- ½ teaspoon garlic powder
- ¼ teaspoon salt
- ¼ teaspoon black pepper
- ¼ cup finely chopped cilantro

Directions:

1. Preheat the air fryer to 400°F.
2. In a medium microwave-safe bowl, melt the butter in the microwave. Lightly brush the outside of the ears of corn with the melted butter.
3. Place the corn into the air fryer basket and cook for 5 minutes, flip the corn, and cook another 5 minutes.
4. Meanwhile, in a medium bowl, mix the yogurt, cheese, paprika, garlic powder, salt, and pepper. Set aside.
5. Carefully remove the corn from the air fryer and let cool 3 minutes. Brush the outside edges with the yogurt mixture and top with fresh chopped cilantro. Serve immediately.

Brussels Sprouts

Serving: 3
Cooking Time: 5 Minutes

Ingredients:

- 1 10-ounce package frozen brussels sprouts, thawed and halved
- 2 teaspoons olive oil
- salt and pepper

Directions:

1. Toss the brussels sprouts and olive oil together.
2. Place them in the air fryer basket and season to taste with salt and pepper.
3. Cook at 360°F for approximately 5minutes, until the edges begin to brown.

Cholula Onion Rings

Servings: 4
Cooking Time: 30 Minutes

Ingredients:

- 1 large Vidalia onion
- ½ cup chickpea flour
- 1/3 cup milk
- 2 tbsp lemon juice
- 2 tbsp Cholula hot sauce
- 1 tsp allspice
- 2/3 cup bread crumbs

Directions:

1. Preheat air fryer to 380°F. Cut ½-inch off the top of the onion's root, then cut into ½-inch thick rings. Set aside. Combine the chickpea flour, milk, lemon juice, hot sauce, and allspice in a bowl. In another bowl, add in breadcrumbs. Submerge each ring into the flour batter until well coated, then dip into the breadcrumbs, and Air Fry for 14 minutes until crispy, turning once. Serve.

Mom´s Potatoes Au Gratin

Servings: 4
Cooking Time: 50 Minutes

Ingredients:

- 4 Yukon Gold potatoes, peeled
- 1cup shredded cheddar cheese
- 2 tbsp grated Parmesan cheese
- 2 garlic cloves, minced
- 1/3 cup heavy cream
- 1/3 cup whole milk
- ½ tsp dried marjoram
- Salt and pepper to taste

Directions:

1. Preheat the air fryer to 350°F. Spray a 7-inch round pan thoroughly with cooking oil. Cut the potatoes into ⅛-inch-thick slices and layer the potatoes inside the pan along with cheddar cheese and garlic. Mix the cream, milk, marjoram, salt, and pepper in a bowl, then slowly pour the mix over the potatoes. Sprinkle with Parmesan and put the pan in the fryer. Bake for 25-35 minutes or until the potatoes are tender, the sauce is bubbling, and the top is golden. Serve warm.

Perfect French Fries

Servings: 3
Cooking Time: 37 Minutes

Ingredients:

- 1 pound Large russet potato(es)
- Vegetable oil or olive oil spray
- ½ teaspoon Table salt

Directions:

1. Cut each potato lengthwise into ¼-inch-thick slices. Cut each of these lengthwise into ¼-inch-thick matchsticks.
2. Set the potato matchsticks in a big bowl of cool water and soak for 5 minutes. Drain in a colander set in the sink, then spread the matchsticks out on paper towels and dry them very well.
3. Preheat the air fryer to 225°F (or 230°F, if that's the closest setting).
4. When the machine is at temperature, arrange the matchsticks in an even layer (if overlapping but not compact) in the basket. Air-fry for 20 minutes, tossing and rearranging the fries twice.
5. Pour the contents of the basket into a big bowl. Increase the air fryer's temperature to 325°F (or 330°F, if that's the closest setting).
6. Generously coat the fries with vegetable or olive oil spray. Toss well, then coat them again to make sure they're covered on all sides, tossing (and maybe spraying) a couple of times to make sure.
7. When the machine is at temperature, pour the fries into the basket and air-fry for 12 minutes, tossing and rearranging the fries at least twice.
8. Increase the machine's temperature to 375°F (or 380°F or 390°F, if one of these is the closest setting). Air-fry for 5 minutes more (from the moment you raise the temperature), tossing and rearranging the fries at least twice to keep them from burning and to make sure they all get an even measure of the heat, until brown and crisp.
9. Pour the contents of the basket into a serving bowl. Toss the fries with the salt and serve hot.

Sweet Potato Curly Fries

Servings: 4
Cooking Time: 10 Minutes

Ingredients:

- 2 medium sweet potatoes, washed
- 2 tablespoons avocado oil
- ¾ teaspoon salt, divided
- 1 medium avocado
- ½ teaspoon garlic powder
- ½ teaspoon paprika
- ¼ teaspoon black pepper
- ½ juice lime
- 3 tablespoons fresh cilantro

Directions:

1. Preheat the air fryer to 400°F.
2. Using a spiralizer, create curly spirals with the sweet potatoes. Keep the pieces about 1½ inches long. Continue until all the potatoes are used.
3. In a large bowl, toss the curly sweet potatoes with the avocado oil and ½ teaspoon of the salt.
4. Place the potatoes in the air fryer basket and cook for 5 minutes; shake and cook another 5 minutes.
5. While cooking, add the avocado, garlic, paprika, pepper, the remaining ¼ teaspoon of salt, lime juice, and cilantro to a blender and process until smooth. Set aside.
6. When cooking completes, remove the fries and serve warm with the lime avocado sauce.

Mexican-style Roasted Corn

Servings: 3
Cooking Time: 14 Minutes

Ingredients:

- 3 tablespoons Butter, melted and cooled
- 2 teaspoons Minced garlic
- ¾ teaspoon Ground cumin
- Up to ¾ teaspoon Red pepper flakes
- ¼ teaspoon Table salt
- 3 Cold 4-inch lengths husked and de-silked corn on the cob
- Minced fresh cilantro leaves
- Crumbled queso fresco

Directions:

1. Preheat the air fryer to 400°F.
2. Mix the melted butter, garlic, cumin, red pepper flakes, and salt in a large zip-closed plastic bag. Add the cold corn pieces, seal the bag, and massage the butter mixture into the surface of the corn.
3. When the machine is at temperature, take the pieces of corn out of the plastic bag and put them in the basket with as much air space between the pieces as possible. Air-fry undisturbed for 14 minutes, until golden brown and maybe even charred in a few small spots.
4. Use kitchen tongs to gently transfer the pieces of corn to a serving platter. Sprinkle each piece with the cilantro and queso fresco. Serve warm.

Five-spice Roasted Sweet Potatoes

Servings: 4
Cooking Time: 12 Minutes

Ingredients:

- ½ teaspoon ground cinnamon
- ¼ teaspoon ground cumin
- ¼ teaspoon paprika
- 1 teaspoon chile powder
- ⅛ teaspoon turmeric
- ½ teaspoon salt (optional)
- freshly ground black pepper
- 2 large sweet potatoes, peeled and cut into ¾-inch cubes (about 3 cups)
- 1 tablespoon olive oil

Directions:

1. In a large bowl, mix together cinnamon, cumin, paprika, chile powder, turmeric, salt, and pepper to taste.
2. Add potatoes and stir well.
3. Drizzle the seasoned potatoes with the olive oil and stir until evenly coated.
4. Place seasoned potatoes in the air fryer baking pan or an ovenproof dish that fits inside your air fryer basket.
5. Cook for 6minutes at 390°F, stop, and stir well.
6. Cook for an additional 6minutes.

Quick Air Fried Potatoes

Servings: 3
Cooking Time: 55 Minutes

Ingredients:

- 3 whole potatoes
- 2 tsp olive oil
- 1 tbsp salt
- 1 tbsp minced garlic
- 1 tsp parsley, chopped
- 4 oz grated Swiss cheese

Directions:

1. Preheat air fryer to 390°F. Prick the potatoes all over using a fork. Drizzle with olive oil all over the skins and rub them with minced garlic, salt, and parsley. Place the potatoes in the frying basket and Bake for 20-25 minutes or until tender. Remove the potatoes from the basket and serve them along with grated Swiss cheese. Serve.

Sesame Carrots And Sugar Snap Peas

Cooking Time: 16 Minutes
Servings: 4

Ingredients:

- 1 pound carrots, peeled sliced on the bias (½-inch slices)
- 1 teaspoon olive oil
- salt and freshly ground black pepper
- ⅓ cup honey
- 1 tablespoon sesame oil
- 1 tablespoon soy sauce
- ½ teaspoon minced fresh ginger
- 4 ounces sugar snap peas (about 1 cup)
- 1½ teaspoons sesame seeds

Directions:

1. Preheat the air fryer to 360°F.
2. Toss the carrots with the olive oil, season with salt and pepper and air-fry for 10 minutes, shaking the basket once or twice during the cooking process.
3. Combine the honey, sesame oil, soy sauce and minced ginger in a large bowl. Add the sugar snap peas and the air-fried carrots to the honey mixture, toss to coat and return everything to the air fryer basket.
4. Turn up the temperature to 400°F and air-fry for an additional 6 minutes, shaking the basket once during the cooking process.
5. Transfer the carrots and sugar snap peas to a serving bowl. Pour the sauce from the bottom of the cooker over the vegetables and sprinkle sesame seeds over top. Serve immediately.

Zucchini Fries

Servings: 3
Cooking Time: 12 Minutes

Ingredients:

- 1 large Zucchini
- ½ cup All-purpose flour or tapioca flour
- 2 Large egg(s), well beaten
- 1 cup Seasoned Italian-style dried bread crumbs (gluten-free, if a concern)
- Olive oil spray

Directions:

1. Preheat the air fryer to 400°F.
2. Trim the zucchini into a long rectangular block, taking off the ends and four "sides" to make this shape. Cut the block lengthwise into ½-inch-thick slices. Lay these slices flat and cut in half widthwise. Slice each of these pieces into ½-inch-thick batons.
3. Set up and fill three shallow soup plates or small pie plates on your counter: one for the flour, one for the beaten egg(s), and one for the bread crumbs.
4. Set a zucchini baton in the flour and turn it several times to coat all sides. Gently shake off any excess flour, then dip it in the egg(s), turning it to coat. Let any excess egg slip back into the rest, then set the baton in the bread crumbs and turn it several times, pressing gently to coat all sides, even the ends. Set aside on a cutting board and continue coating the remainder of the batons in the same way.
5. Lightly coat the batons on all sides with olive oil spray. Set them in two flat layers in the basket, the top layer at a 90-degree angle to the bottom one, with a little air space between the batons in each layer. In the end, the whole thing will look like a crosshatch pattern. Air-fry undisturbed for 6 minutes.
6. Use kitchen tongs to gently rearrange the batons so that any covered parts are now uncovered. The batons no longer need to be in a crosshatch pattern. Continue air-frying undisturbed for 6 minutes, or until lightly browned and crisp.
7. Gently pour the contents of the basket onto a wire rack. Spread the batons out and cool for only a minute or two before serving.

Crunchy Roasted Potatoes

Servings: 5
Cooking Time: 25 Minutes

Ingredients:

- 2 pounds Small (1- to 1½-inch-diameter) red, white, or purple potatoes
- 2 tablespoons Olive oil
- 2 teaspoons Table salt
- ¾ teaspoon Garlic powder
- ½ teaspoon Ground black pepper

Directions:

1. Preheat the air fryer to 400°F.
2. Toss the potatoes, oil, salt, garlic powder, and pepper in a large bowl until the spuds are evenly and thoroughly coated.
3. When the machine is at temperature, pour the potatoes into the basket, spreading them into an even layer (although they may be stacked on top of each other). Air-fry for 25 minutes, tossing twice, until the potatoes are tender but crunchy.
4. Pour the contents of the basket into a serving bowl. Cool for 5 minutes before serving.

Roasted Cauliflower With Garlic And Capers

Servings: 3
Cooking Time: 10 Minutes

Ingredients:

- 3 cups (about 15 ounces) 1-inch cauliflower florets
- 2 tablespoons Olive oil
- 1½ tablespoons Drained and rinsed capers, chopped
- 2 teaspoons Minced garlic
- ¼ teaspoon Table salt
- Up to ¼ teaspoon Red pepper flakes

Directions:

1. Preheat the air fryer to 375°F .
2. Stir the cauliflower florets, olive oil, capers, garlic, salt, and red pepper flakes in a large bowl until the florets are evenly coated.
3. When the machine is at temperature, put the florets in the basket, spreading them out to as close to one layer as you can. Air-fry for 10 minutes, tossing once to get any covered pieces exposed to the air currents, until tender and lightly browned.
4. Dump the contents of the basket into a serving bowl or onto a serving platter. Cool for a minute or two before serving.

VEGETARIANS RECIPES

Broccoli Cheddar Stuffed Potatoes

Servings: 2
Cooking Time: 42 Minutes

Ingredients:

- 2 large russet potatoes, scrubbed
- 1 tablespoon olive oil
- salt and freshly ground black pepper
- 2 tablespoons butter
- ¼ cup sour cream
- 3 tablespoons half-and-half (or milk)
- 1¼ cups grated Cheddar cheese, divided
- ¾ teaspoon salt
- freshly ground black pepper
- 1 cup frozen baby broccoli florets, thawed and drained

Directions:

1. Preheat the air fryer to 400°F.
2. Rub the potatoes all over with olive oil and season generously with salt and freshly ground black pepper. Transfer the potatoes into the air fryer basket and air-fry for 30 minutes, turning the potatoes over halfway through the cooking process.
3. Remove the potatoes from the air fryer and let them rest for 5 minutes. Cut a large oval out of the top of both potatoes. Leaving half an inch of potato flesh around the edge of the potato, scoop the inside of the potato out and into a large bowl to prepare the potato filling. Mash the scooped potato filling with a fork and add the butter, sour cream, half-and-half, 1 cup of the grated Cheddar cheese, salt and pepper to taste. Mix well and then fold in the broccoli florets.
4. Stuff the hollowed out potato shells with the potato and broccoli mixture. Mound the filling high in the potatoes – you will have more filling than room in the potato shells.
5. Transfer the stuffed potatoes back to the air fryer basket and air-fry at 360°F for 10 minutes. Sprinkle the remaining Cheddar cheese on top of each stuffed potato, lower the heat to 330°F and air-fry for an additional minute or two to melt cheese.

Mushroom Bolognese Casserole

Servings: 4
Cooking Time: 20 Minutes

Ingredients:

- 1 cup canned diced tomatoes
- 2 garlic cloves, minced
- 1 tsp onion powder
- ¾ tsp dried basil
- ¾ tsp dried oregano
- 1 cup chopped mushrooms
- 16 oz cooked spaghetti

Directions:

1. Preheat air fryer to 400°F. Whisk the tomatoes and their juices, garlic, onion powder, basil, oregano, and mushrooms in a baking pan. Cover with aluminum foil and Bake for 6 minutes. Slide out the pan and add the cooked spaghetti; stir to coat. Cover with aluminum foil and Bake for 3 minutes until and bubbly. Serve and enjoy!

Eggplant Parmesan

Servings: 4
Cooking Time: 8 Minutes Per Batch

Ingredients:

- 1 medium eggplant, 6–8 inches long
- salt
- 1 large egg
- 1 tablespoon water
- ⅔ cup panko breadcrumbs
- ⅓ cup grated Parmesan cheese, plus more for serving
- 1 tablespoon Italian seasoning
- ¾ teaspoon oregano
- oil for misting or cooking spray
- 1 24-ounce jar marinara sauce
- 8 ounces spaghetti, cooked
- pepper

Directions:

1. Preheat air fryer to 390°F.
2. Leaving peel intact, cut eggplant into 8 round slices about ¾-inch thick. Salt to taste.
3. Beat egg and water in a shallow dish.
4. In another shallow dish, combine panko, Parmesan, Italian seasoning, and oregano.
5. Dip eggplant slices in egg wash and then crumbs, pressing lightly to coat.
6. Mist slices with oil or cooking spray.
7. Place 4 eggplant slices in air fryer basket and cook for 8 minutes, until brown and crispy.
8. While eggplant is cooking, heat marinara sauce.
9. Repeat step 7 to cook remaining eggplant slices.
10. To serve, place cooked spaghetti on plates and top with marinara and eggplant slices. At the table, pass extra Parmesan cheese and freshly ground black pepper.

Hearty Salad

Servings: 2
Cooking Time: 15 Minutes

Ingredients:

- 5 oz cauliflower, cut into florets
- 2 grated carrots
- 1 tbsp olive oil
- 1 tbsp lemon juice
- 2 tbsp raisins
- 2 tbsp roasted pepitas
- 2 tbsp diced red onion
- ¼ cup mayonnaise
- 1/8 tsp black pepper
- 1 tsp cumin
- ½ tsp chia seeds
- ½ tsp sesame seeds

Directions:

1. Preheat air fryer at 350°F. Combine the cauliflower, cumin, olive oil, black pepper and lemon juice in a bowl, place it in the frying basket, and Bake for 5 minutes. Transfer it to a serving dish. Toss in the remaining ingredients. Let chill covered in the fridge until ready to use. Serve sprinkled with sesame and chia seeds.

Basic Fried Tofu

Servings: 4
Cooking Time: 17 Minutes

Ingredients:

- 14 ounces extra-firm tofu, drained and pressed
- 1 tablespoon sesame oil
- 2 tablespoons low-sodium soy sauce
- ¼ cup rice vinegar
- 1 tablespoon fresh grated ginger
- 1 clove garlic, minced
- 3 tablespoons cornstarch
- ¼ teaspoon black pepper
- ⅛ teaspoon salt

Directions:

1. Cut the tofu into 16 cubes. Set aside in a glass container with a lid.
2. In a medium bowl, mix the sesame oil, soy sauce, rice vinegar, ginger, and garlic. Pour over the tofu and secure the lid. Place in the refrigerator to marinate for an hour.
3. Preheat the air fryer to 350°F.
4. In a small bowl, mix the cornstarch, black pepper, and salt.
5. Transfer the tofu to a large bowl and discard the leftover marinade. Pour the cornstarch mixture over the tofu and toss until all the pieces are coated.
6. Liberally spray the air fryer basket with olive oil mist and set the tofu pieces inside. Allow space between the tofu so it can cook evenly. Cook in batches if necessary.
7. Cook 15 to 17 minutes, shaking the basket every 5 minutes to allow the tofu to cook evenly on all sides. When it's done cooking, the tofu will be crisped and browned on all sides.
8. Remove the tofu from the air fryer basket and serve warm.

Arancini With Marinara

Servings: 6
Cooking Time: 15 Minutes

Ingredients:

- 2 cups cooked rice
- 1 cup grated Parmesan cheese
- 1 egg, whisked
- ¼ teaspoon dried thyme
- ½ teaspoon dried oregano
- ½ teaspoon dried basil
- ½ teaspoon dried parsley
- 1 teaspoon salt
- ¼ teaspoon paprika
- 1 cup breadcrumbs
- 4 ounces mozzarella, cut into 24 cubes
- 2 cups marinara sauce

Directions:

1. In a large bowl, mix together the rice, Parmesan cheese, and egg.
2. In another bowl, mix together the thyme, oregano, basil, parsley, salt, paprika, and breadcrumbs.
3. Form 24 rice balls with the rice mixture. Use your thumb to make an indentation in the center and stuff 1 cube of mozzarella in the center of the rice; close the ball around the cheese.
4. Roll the rice balls in the seasoned breadcrumbs until all are coated.
5. Preheat the air fryer to 400°F.
6. Place the rice balls in the air fryer basket and coat with cooking spray. Cook for 8 minutes, shake the basket, and cook another 7 minutes.
7. Heat the marinara sauce in a saucepan until warm. Serve sauce as a dip for arancini.

Mushroom And Fried Onion Quesadilla

Servings: 2
Cooking Time: 33 Minutes

Ingredients:

- 1 onion, sliced
- 2 tablespoons butter, melted
- 10 ounces button mushrooms, sliced
- 2 tablespoons Worcestershire sauce
- salt and freshly ground black pepper
- 4 (8-inch) flour tortillas
- 2 cups grated Fontina cheese
- vegetable or olive oil

Directions:

1. Preheat the air fryer to 400°F.
2. Toss the onion slices with the melted butter and transfer them to the air fryer basket. Air-fry at 400°F for 15 minutes, shaking the basket several times during the cooking process. Add the mushrooms and Worcestershire sauce to the onions and stir to combine. Air-fry at 400°F for an additional 10 minutes. Season with salt and freshly ground black pepper.
3. Lay two of the tortillas on a cutting board. Top each tortilla with ½ cup of the grated cheese, half of the onion and mushroom mixture and then finally another ½ cup of the cheese. Place the remaining tortillas on top of the cheese and press down firmly.
4. Brush the air fryer basket with a little oil. Place a quesadilla in the basket and brush the top with a little oil. Secure the top tortilla to the bottom with three toothpicks and air-fry at 400°F for 5 minutes. Flip the quesadilla over by inverting it onto a plate and sliding it back into the basket. Remove the toothpicks and brush the other side with oil. Air-fry for an additional 3 minutes.
5. Invert the quesadilla onto a cutting board and cut it into 4 or 6 triangles. Serve immediately.

Spaghetti Squash And Kale Fritters With Pomodoro Sauce

Servings: 3
Cooking Time: 45 Minutes

Ingredients:

- 1½-pound spaghetti squash (about half a large or a whole small squash)
- olive oil
- ½ onion, diced
- ½ red bell pepper, diced
- 2 cloves garlic, minced
- 4 cups coarsely chopped kale
- salt and freshly ground black pepper
- 1 egg
- ⅓ cup breadcrumbs, divided*
- ⅓ cup grated Parmesan cheese
- ½ teaspoon dried rubbed sage
- pinch nutmeg
- Pomodoro Sauce:
- 2 tablespoons olive oil
- ½ onion, chopped
- 1 to 2 cloves garlic, minced
- 1 (28-ounce) can peeled tomatoes
- ¼ cup red wine
- 1 teaspoon Italian seasoning
- 2 tablespoons chopped fresh basil, plus more for garnish
- salt and freshly ground black pepper
- ½ teaspoon sugar (optional)

Directions:

1. Preheat the air fryer to 370°F.
2. Cut the spaghetti squash in half lengthwise and remove the seeds. Rub the inside of the squash with olive oil and season with salt and pepper. Place the squash, cut side up, into the air fryer basket and air-fry for 30 minutes, flipping the squash over halfway through the cooking process.
3. While the squash is cooking, Preheat a large sauté pan over medium heat on the stovetop. Add a little olive oil and sauté the onions for 3 minutes, until they start to soften. Add the red pepper and garlic and continue to sauté for an additional 4 minutes. Add the kale and season with salt and pepper. Cook for 2 more minutes, or until the kale is soft. Transfer the mixture to a large bowl and let it cool.
4. While the squash continues to cook, make the Pomodoro sauce. Preheat the large sauté pan again over medium heat on the stovetop. Add the olive oil and sauté the onion and garlic for 2 to 3 minutes, until the onion begins to soften. Crush the canned tomatoes with your hands and add them to the pan along with the red wine and Italian seasoning and simmer for 20 minutes. Add the basil and season to taste with salt, pepper and sugar (if using).
5. When the spaghetti squash has finished cooking, use a fork to scrape the inside flesh of the squash onto a sheet pan. Spread the squash out and let it cool.
6. Once cool, add the spaghetti squash to the kale mixture, along with the egg, breadcrumbs, Parmesan cheese, sage, nutmeg, salt and freshly ground black pepper. Stir to combine well and then divide the mixture into 6 thick portions. You can shape the portions into patties, but I prefer to keep them a little random and unique in shape. Spray or brush the fritters with olive oil.
7. Preheat the air fryer to 370°F.
8. Brush the air fryer basket with a little olive oil and transfer the fritters to the basket. Air-fry the squash and kale fritters at 370°F for 15 minutes, flipping them over halfway through the cooking process.
9. Serve the fritters warm with the Pomodoro sauce spooned over the top or pooled on your plate. Garnish with the fresh basil leaves.

Spring Veggie Empanadas

Servings: 4
Cooking Time: 75 Minutes

Ingredients:

- 10 empanada pastry discs
- 1 tbsp olive oil
- 1 shallot, minced
- 1 garlic clove, minced
- ½ cup whole milk
- 1 cup chopped broccoli
- ½ cup chopped cauliflower
- ½ cup diced carrots
- ¼ cup diced celery
- ⅛ tsp ground nutmeg
- 1 tsp cumin powder
- 1 tsp minced ginger
- 1 egg

Directions:

1. Melt the olive oil in a pot over medium heat. Stir in shallot and garlic and cook through for 1 minute. Next, add 1 tablespoon of flour and continue stirring. Whisk in milk, then lower the heat. After that, add broccoli, cauliflower, carrots, celery, cumin powder, pepper, ginger, and nutmeg. Cook for 2 minutes then remove from the heat. Allow to cool for 5 minutes.
2. Preheat air fryer to 350°F. Lightly flour a flat work surface and turn out the pastry discs. Scoop ¼ of the vegetables in the center of each circle. Whisk the egg and 1 teaspoon of water in a small bowl and brush the entire edge of the circle with the egg wash and fold the dough over the filling into a half-moon shape. Crimp the edge with a fork to seal. Arrange the patties in a single layer in the frying basket and bake for 12 minutes. Flip the patties and bake for another 10 to 12 minutes until the outside crust is golden. Serve immediately and enjoy.

Mushroom-rice Stuffed Bell Peppers

Servings: 4
Cooking Time: 30 Minutes

Ingredients:

- 4 red bell peppers, tops sliced
- 1 ½ cups cooked rice
- ¼ cup chopped leeks
- ¼ cup sliced mushrooms
- ¾ cup tomato sauce
- Salt and pepper to taste
- ¾ cup shredded mozzarella
- 2 tbsp parsley, chopped

Directions:

1. Fill a large pot of water and heat on high until it boils. Remove seeds and membranes from the peppers. Carefully place peppers into the boiling water for 5 minutes. Remove and set aside to cool. Mix together rice, leeks, mushrooms, tomato sauce, parsley, salt, and pepper in a large bowl. Stuff each pepper with the rice mixture. Top with mozzarella.
2. Preheat air fryer to 350°F. Arrange the peppers on the greased frying basket and Bake for 10 minutes. Serve.

Breaded Avocado Tacos

Servings: 3
Cooking Time: 20 Minutes

Ingredients:

- 2 tomatoes, diced
- ¼ cup diced red onion
- 1 jalapeño, finely diced
- 1 tbsp lime juice
- 1 tsp lime zest
- ¼ cup chopped cilantro
- 1 tsp salt
- 1 egg
- 2 tbsp milk
- 1 cup crumbs
- ¼ cup of almond flour
- 1 avocado, sliced into fries
- 6 flour tortillas
- 1 cup coleslaw mix

Directions:

1. In a bowl, combine the tomatoes, jalapeño, red onion, lime juice, lime zest, cilantro, and salt. Let chill the pico de gallo covered in the fridge until ready to use.
2. Preheat air fryer at 375°F. In a small bowl, beat egg and milk. In another bowl, add breadcrumbs. Dip avocado slices in the egg mixture, then dredge them in the mixed almond flour and breadcrumbs. Place avocado slices in the greased frying basket and Air Fry for 5 minutes. Add 2 avocado fries to each tortilla. Top each with coleslaw mix. Serve immediately.

Tacos

Servings: 24
Cooking Time: 8 Minutes Per Batch

Ingredients:

- 1 24-count package 4-inch corn tortillas
- 1½ cups refried beans (about ¾ of a 15-ounce can)
- 4 ounces sharp Cheddar cheese, grated
- ½ cup salsa
- oil for misting or cooking spray

Directions:

1. Preheat air fryer to 390°F.
2. Wrap refrigerated tortillas in damp paper towels and microwave for 30 to 60 seconds to warm. If necessary, rewarm tortillas as you go to keep them soft enough to fold without breaking.
3. Working with one tortilla at a time, top with 1 tablespoon of beans, 1 tablespoon of grated cheese, and 1 teaspoon of salsa. Fold over and press down very gently on the center. Press edges firmly all around to seal. Spray both sides with oil or cooking spray.
4. Cooking in two batches, place half the tacos in the air fryer basket. To cook 12 at a time, you may need to stand them upright and lean some against the sides of basket. It's okay if they're crowded as long as you leave a little room for air to circulate around them.
5. Cook for 8 minutes or until golden brown and crispy.
6. Repeat steps 4 and 5 to cook remaining tacos.

Mexican Twice Air-fried Sweet Potatoes

Servings: 2
Cooking Time: 42 Minutes

Ingredients:

- 2 large sweet potatoes
- olive oil
- salt and freshly ground black pepper
- ⅓ cup diced red onion
- ⅓ cup diced red bell pepper
- ½ cup canned black beans, drained and rinsed
- ½ cup corn kernels, fresh or frozen
- ½ teaspoon chili powder
- 1½ cups grated pepper jack cheese, divided
- Jalapeño peppers, sliced

Directions:

1. Preheat the air fryer to 400°F.
2. Rub the outside of the sweet potatoes with olive oil and season with salt and freshly ground black pepper. Transfer the potatoes into the air fryer basket and air-fry at 400°F for 30 minutes, rotating the potatoes a few times during the cooking process.
3. While the potatoes are air-frying, start the potato filling. Preheat a large sauté pan over medium heat on the stovetop. Add the onion and pepper and sauté for a few minutes, until the vegetables start to soften. Add the black beans, corn, and chili powder and sauté for another 3 minutes. Set the mixture aside.
4. Remove the sweet potatoes from the air fryer and let them rest for 5 minutes. Slice off one inch of the flattest side of both potatoes. Scrape the potato flesh out of the potatoes, leaving half an inch of potato flesh around the edge of the potato. Place all the potato flesh into a large bowl and mash it with a fork. Add the black bean mixture and 1 cup of the pepper jack cheese to the mashed sweet potatoes. Season with salt and freshly ground black pepper and mix well. Stuff the hollowed out potato shells with the black bean and sweet potato mixture, mounding the filling high in the potatoes.
5. Transfer the stuffed potatoes back into the air fryer basket and air-fry at 370°F for 10 minutes. Sprinkle the remaining cheese on top of each stuffed potato, lower the heat to 340°F and air-fry for an additional 2 minutes to melt the cheese. Top with a couple slices of Jalapeño pepper and serve warm with a green salad.

Vegetarian Paella

Servings: 3
Cooking Time: 50 Minutes

Ingredients:

- ½ cup chopped artichoke hearts
- ½ sliced red bell peppers
- 4 mushrooms, thinly sliced
- ½ cup canned diced tomatoes
- ½ cup canned chickpeas
- 3 tbsp hot sauce
- 2 tbsp lemon juice
- 1 tbsp allspice
- 1 cup rice

Directions:

1. Preheat air fryer to 400°F. Combine the artichokes, peppers, mushrooms, tomatoes and their juices, chickpeas, hot sauce, lemon juice, and allspice in a baking pan. Roast for 10 minutes. Pour in rice and 2 cups of boiling water, cover with aluminum foil, and Roast for 22 minutes. Discard the foil and Roast for 3 minutes until the top is crisp. Let cool slightly before stirring. Serve.

Meatless Kimchi Bowls

Servings:4
Cooking Time: 20 Minutes

Ingredients:

- 2 cups canned chickpeas
- 1 carrot, julienned
- 6 scallions, sliced
- 1 zucchini, diced
- 2 tbsp coconut aminos
- 2 tsp sesame oil
- 1 tsp rice vinegar
- 2 tsp granulated sugar
- 1 tbsp gochujang
- ¼ tsp salt
- ½ cup kimchi
- 2 tsp roasted sesame seeds

Directions:

1. Preheat air fryer to 350ºF. Combine all ingredients, except for the kimchi, 2 scallions, and sesame seeds, in a baking pan. Place the pan in the frying basket and Air Fry for 6 minutes. Toss in kimchi and cook for 2 more minutes. Divide between 2 bowls and garnish with the remaining scallions and sesame seeds. Serve immediately.

Curried Cauliflower

Servings: 2
Cooking Time: 30 Minutes

Ingredients:

- 1 cup canned diced tomatoes
- 2 cups milk
- 2 tbsp lime juice
- 1 tbsp allspice
- 1 tbsp curry powder
- 1 tsp ground ginger
- ½ tsp ground cumin
- 12 oz frozen cauliflower
- 16 oz cheddar cheese, cubed
- ¼ cup chopped cilantro

Directions:

1. Preheat air fryer to 375°F. Combine the tomatoes and their juices, milk, lime juice, allspice, curry powder, ginger, and cumin in a baking pan. Toss in cauliflower and cheddar cheese until coated. Roast for 15 minutes, stir and Roast for another 10 minutes until bubbly. Scatter with cilantro before serving.

Quinoa & Black Bean Stuffed Peppers

Servings: 4
Cooking Time: 30 Minutes

Ingredients:

- ½ cup vegetable broth
- ½ cup quinoa
- 1 can black beans
- ½ cup diced red onion
- 1 garlic clove, minced
- ½ tsp salt
- ½ tsp ground cumin
- ¼ tsp paprika
- ¼ tsp ancho chili powder
- 4 bell peppers, any color
- ½ cup grated cheddar
- ¼ cup chopped cilantro
- ½ cup red enchilada sauce

Directions:

1. Add vegetable broth and quinoa to a small saucepan over medium heat. Bring to a boil, then cover and let it simmer for 5 minutes. Turn off the heat.
2. Preheat air fryer to 350°F. Transfer quinoa to a medium bowl and stir in black beans, onion, red enchilada sauce, ancho chili powder, garlic, salt, cumin, and paprika. Cut the top ¼-inch off the bell peppers. Remove seeds and membranes. Scoop quinoa filling into each pepper and top with cheddar cheese. Transfer peppers to the frying basket and bake for 10 minutes until peppers are soft and filling is heated through. Garnish with cilantro. Serve warm along with salsa. Enjoy!

Fried Potatoes With Bell Peppers

Servings: 4
Cooking Time: 30 Minutes

Ingredients:

- 3 russet potatoes, cubed
- 1 tbsp canola oil
- 1 tbsp olive oil
- 1 tsp paprika
- Salt and pepper to taste
- 1 chopped shallot
- ½ chopped red bell peppers
- ½ diced yellow bell peppers

Directions:

1. Preheat air fryer to 370°F. Whisk the canola oil, olive oil, paprika, salt, and pepper in a bowl. Toss in the potatoes to coat. Place the potatoes in the air fryer and Bake for 20 minutes, shaking the basket periodically. Top the potatoes with shallot and bell peppers and cook for an additional 3-4 minutes or until the potatoes are cooked through and the peppers are soft. Serve warm.

BEEF ,PORK & LAMB RECIPES

Cheeseburger Sliders With Pickle Sauce

Servings: 4
Cooking Time: 20 Minutes

Ingredients:

- 4 iceberg lettuce leaves, each halved lengthwise
- 2 red onion slices, rings separated
- ¼ cup shredded Swiss cheese
- 1 lb ground beef
- 1 tbsp Dijon mustard
- Salt and pepper to taste
- ¼ tsp shallot powder
- 2 tbsp mayonnaise
- 2 tsp ketchup
- ½ tsp mustard powder
- ½ tsp dill pickle juice
- ⅛ tsp onion powder
- ⅛ tsp garlic powder
- ⅛ tsp sweet paprika
- 8 tomato slices
- ½ cucumber, thinly sliced

Directions:

1. In a large bowl, use your hands to mix beef, Swiss cheese, mustard, salt, shallot, and black pepper. Do not overmix. Form 8 patties ½-inch thick. Mix together mayonnaise, ketchup, mustard powder, pickle juice, onion and garlic powder, and paprika in a medium bowl. Stir until smooth.
2. Preheat air fryer to 400°F. Place the sliders in the greased frying basket and Air Fry for about 8-10 minutes, flipping once until preferred doneness. Serve on top of lettuce halves with a slice of tomato, a slider, onion, a smear of special sauce, and cucumber.

Pork Tenderloin With Apples & Celery

Servings: 4
Cooking Time: 30 Minutes

Ingredients:

- 1 lb pork tenderloin, cut into 4 pieces
- 2 Granny Smith apples, sliced
- 1 tbsp butter, melted
- 2 tsp olive oil
- 3 celery stalks, sliced
- 1 onion, sliced
- 2 tsp dried thyme
- 1/3 cup apple juice

Directions:

1. Preheat air fryer to 400°F. Brush olive oil and butter all over the pork, then toss the pork, apples, celery, onion, thyme, and apple juice in a bowl and mix well. Put the bowl in the air fryer and Roast for 15-19 minutes until the pork is cooked through and the apples and veggies are soft, stirring once during cooking. Serve warm.

Sage Pork With Potatoes

Servings: 4
Cooking Time: 30 Minutes

Ingredients:

- 2 cups potatoes
- 2 tsp olive oil
- 1 lb pork tenderloin, cubed
- 1 onion, chopped
- 1 red bell pepper, chopped
- 2 garlic cloves, minced
- ½ tsp dried sage
- ½ tsp fennel seeds, crushed
- 2 tbsp chicken broth

Directions:

1. Preheat air fryer to 370°F. Add the potatoes and olive oil to a bowl and toss to coat. Transfer them to the frying basket and Air Fry for 15 minutes. Remove the bowl. Add the pork, onion, red bell pepper, garlic, sage, and fennel seeds, to the potatoes, add chicken broth and stir gently. Return the bowl to the frying basket and cook for 10 minutes. Be sure to shake the basket at least once. The pork should be cooked through and the potatoes soft and crispy. Serve immediately.

Stuffed Pork Chops

Servings: 4
Cooking Time: 12 Minutes

Ingredients:

- 4 boneless pork chops
- ½ teaspoon salt
- ½ teaspoon black pepper
- ¼ teaspoon paprika
- 1 cup frozen spinach, defrosted and squeezed dry
- 2 cloves garlic, minced
- 2 ounces cream cheese
- ¼ cup grated Parmesan cheese
- 1 tablespoon extra-virgin olive oil

Directions:

1. Pat the pork chops with a paper towel. Make a slit in the side of each pork chop to create a pouch.
2. Season the pork chops with the salt, pepper, and paprika.
3. In a small bowl, mix together the spinach, garlic, cream cheese, and Parmesan cheese.
4. Divide the mixture into fourths and stuff the pork chop pouches. Secure the pouches with toothpicks.
5. Preheat the air fryer to 400°F.
6. Place the stuffed pork chops in the air fryer basket and spray liberally with cooking spray. Cook for 6 minutes, flip and coat with more cooking spray, and cook another 6 minutes. Check to make sure the meat is cooked to an internal temperature of 145°F. Cook the pork chops in batches, as needed.

Honey Mustard Pork Roast

Servings:4
Cooking Time: 50 Minutes

Ingredients:

- 1 boneless pork loin roast
- 2 tbsp Dijon mustard
- 2 tsp olive oil
- 1 tsp honey
- 1 garlic clove, minced
- Salt and pepper to taste
- 1 tsp dried rosemary

Directions:

1. Preheat air fryer to 350ºF. Whisk all ingredients in a bowl. Massage into loin on all sides. Place the loin in the frying basket and Roast for 40 minutes, turning once. Let sit onto a cutting board for 5 minutes before slicing. Serve.

Easy Carnitas

Servings: 3
Cooking Time: 25 Minutes

Ingredients:

- 1½ pounds Boneless country-style pork ribs, cut into 2-inch pieces
- ¼ cup Orange juice
- 2 tablespoons Brine from a jar of pickles, any type, even pickled jalapeño rings (gluten-free, if a concern)
- 2 teaspoons Minced garlic
- 2 teaspoons Minced fresh oregano leaves
- ¾ teaspoon Ground cumin
- ¾ teaspoon Table salt
- ¾ teaspoon Ground black pepper

Directions:

1. Mix the country-style pork rib pieces, orange juice, pickle brine, garlic, oregano, cumin, salt, and pepper in a large bowl. Cover and refrigerate for at least 2 hours or up to 10 hours, stirring the mixture occasionally.
2. Preheat the air fryer to 400°F. Set the rib pieces in their bowl on the counter as the machine heats.
3. Use kitchen tongs to transfer the rib pieces to the basket, arranging them in one layer. Some may touch. Air-fry for 25 minutes, turning and rearranging the pieces at the 10- and 20-minute marks to make sure all surfaces have been exposed to the air currents, until browned and sizzling.
4. Use clean kitchen tongs to transfer the rib pieces to a wire rack. Cool for a couple of minutes before serving.

Country-style Pork Ribs

Servings:4
Cooking Time: 50 Minutes

Ingredients:

- 1 tsp smoked paprika
- 1 tsp ground cumin
- 1 tsp garlic powder
- 1 tsp onion powder
- 1 tbsp honey
- ½ tsp ground mustard
- Salt and pepper to taste
- 2 tbsp olive oil
- 1 tbsp fresh orange juice
- 2 lb country-style pork ribs

Directions:

1. Preheat air fryer to 350ºF. Combine all spices and honey in a bowl. In another bowl, whisk olive oil and orange juice and massage onto pork ribs. Sprinkle with the spice mixture. Place the pork ribs in the frying basket and Air Fry for 40 minutes, flipping every 10 minutes. Serve.

Garlic-buttered Rib Eye Steak

Servings: 2
Cooking Time: 25 Minutes

Ingredients:

- 1 lb rib eye steak
- Salt and pepper to taste
- 1 tbsp butter
- 1 tsp paprika
- 1 tbsp chopped rosemary
- 2 garlic cloves, minced
- 2 tbsp chopped parsley
- 1 tbsp chopped mint

Directions:

1. Preheat air fryer to 400°F. Sprinkle salt and pepper on both sides of the rib eye. Transfer the rib eye to the greased frying basket, then top with butter, mint, paprika, rosemary, and garlic. Bake for 6 minutes, then flip the steak. Bake for another 6 minutes. For medium-rare, the steak needs to reach an internal temperature of 140°F. Allow resting for 5 minutes before slicing. Serve sprinkled with parsley and enjoy!

Wasabi Pork Medallions

Servings: 4
Cooking Time: 20 Minutes + Marinate Time

Ingredients:

- 1 lb pork medallions
- 1 cup soy sauce
- 1 tbsp mirin
- ½ cup olive oil
- 3 cloves garlic, crushed
- 1 tsp fresh grated ginger
- 1 tsp wasabi paste
- 1 tbsp brown sugar

Directions:

1. Place all ingredients, except for the pork, in a resealable bag and shake to combine. Add the pork medallions to the bag, shake again, and place in the fridge to marinate for 2 hours. Preheat air fryer to 360°F. Remove pork medallions from the marinade and place them in the frying basket in rows. Air Fry for 14-16 minutes or until the medallions are cooked through and juicy. Serve.

Spiced Beef Empanadas

Servings: 4
Cooking Time: 35 Minutes

Ingredients:

- 2 tbsp olive oil
- 6 oz ground beef
- 1 shallot, diced
- ½ tsp ground cumin
- ½ tsp nutmeg
- ½ tsp ground cloves
- 1 pinch of brown sugar
- 2 tsp red chili powder
- 4 empanada dough shells

Directions:

1. Preheat air fryer to 350°F. Warm the olive oil in a saucepan over medium heat. Crumble and cook the ground beef for 4-5 minutes. Add in the shallot, cumin, nutmeg, chili powder, and clove and stir-fry for 3 minutes. Kill the heat and let the mixture cool slightly. Divide the beef mixture between the empanada shells. Fold the empanada shells over and use a fork to seal the edges. Sprinkle brown sugar over. Place the empanadas in the foil-lined frying basket and Bake for 15 minutes. Halfway through, flip the empanadas. Cook them until golden. Serve and enjoy!

Calf's Liver

Servings: 4
Cooking Time: 5 Minutes

Ingredients:

- 1 pound sliced calf's liver
- salt and pepper
- 2 eggs
- 2 tablespoons milk
- ½ cup whole wheat flour
- 1½ cups panko breadcrumbs
- ½ cup plain breadcrumbs
- ½ teaspoon salt
- ¼ teaspoon pepper
- oil for misting or cooking spray

Directions:

1. Cut liver slices crosswise into strips about ½-inch wide. Sprinkle with salt and pepper to taste.
2. Beat together egg and milk in a shallow dish.
3. Place wheat flour in a second shallow dish.
4. In a third shallow dish, mix together panko, plain breadcrumbs, ½ teaspoon salt, and ¼ teaspoon pepper.
5. Preheat air fryer to 390°F.
6. Dip liver strips in flour, egg wash, and then breadcrumbs, pressing in coating slightly to make crumbs stick.
7. Cooking half the liver at a time, place strips in air fryer basket in a single layer, close but not touching. Cook at 390°F for 5 minutes or until done to your preference.
8. Repeat step 7 to cook remaining liver.

Crispy Five-spice Pork Belly

Servings: 6
Cooking Time: 60-75 Minutes

Ingredients:

- 1½ pounds Pork belly with skin
- 3 tablespoons Shaoxing (Chinese cooking rice wine), dry sherry, or white grape juice
- 1½ teaspoons Granulated white sugar
- ¾ teaspoon Five-spice powder (see the headnote)
- 1¼ cups Coarse sea salt or kosher salt

Directions:

1. Preheat the air fryer to 350°F .
2. Set the pork belly skin side up on a cutting board. Use a meat fork to make dozens and dozens of tiny holes all across the surface of the skin. You can hardly make too many holes. These will allow the skin to bubble up and keep it from becoming hard as it roasts.
3. Turn the pork belly over so that one of its longer sides faces you. Make four evenly spaced vertical slits in the meat. The slits should go about halfway into the meat toward the fat.
4. Mix the Shaoxing or its substitute, sugar, and five-spice powder in a small bowl until the sugar dissolves. Massage this mixture across the meat and into the cuts.
5. Turn the pork belly over again. Blot dry any moisture on the skin. Make a double-thickness aluminum foil tray by setting two 10-inch-long pieces of foil on top of another. Set the pork belly skin side up in the center of this tray. Fold the sides of the tray up toward the pork, crimping the foil as you work to make a high-sided case all around the pork belly. Seal the foil to the meat on all sides so that only the skin is exposed.
6. Pour the salt onto the skin and pat it down and in place to create a crust. Pick up the foil tray with the pork in it and set it in the basket.
7. Air-fry undisturbed for 35 minutes for a small batch, 45 minutes for a medium batch, or 50 minutes for a large batch.
8. Remove the foil tray with the pork belly still in it. Warning: The foil tray is full of scalding-hot fat. Discard the fat in the tray (not down the drain!), as well as the tray itself. Transfer the pork belly to a cutting board.
9. Raise the air fryer temperature to 375°F (or 380°F or 390°F, if one of these is the closest setting). Brush the salt crust off the pork, removing any visible salt from the sides of the meat, too.
10. When the machine is at temperature, return the pork belly skin side up to the basket. Air-fry undisturbed for 25 minutes, or until crisp and very well browned. If the machine is at 390°F, you may be able to shave 5 minutes off the cooking time so that the skin doesn't blacken.
11. Use a nonstick-safe spatula, and perhaps a silicone baking mitt, to transfer the pork belly to a wire rack. Cool for 10 minutes before serving.

Homemade Pork Gyoza

Servings: 4
Cooking Time: 50 Minutes

Ingredients:

- 8 wonton wrappers
- 4 oz ground pork, browned
- 1 green apple
- 1 tsp rice vinegar
- 1 tbsp vegetable oil
- ½ tbsp oyster sauce
- 1 tbsp soy sauce
- A pinch of white pepper

Directions:

1. Preheat air fryer to 350°F. Combine the oyster sauce, soy sauce, rice vinegar, and white pepper in a small bowl. Add in the pork and stir thoroughly. Peel and core the apple, and slice into small cubes. Add the apples to the meat mixture, and combine thoroughly. Divide the filling between the wonton wrappers. Wrap the wontons into triangles and seal with a bit of water. Brush the wrappers with vegetable oil. Place them in the greased frying basket. Bake for 25 minutes until crispy golden brown on the outside and juicy and delicious on the inside. Serve.

Peppered Steak Bites

Servings: 4
Cooking Time: 14 Minutes

Ingredients:

- 1 pound sirloin steak, cut into 1-inch cubes
- ½ teaspoon coarse sea salt
- 1 teaspoon coarse black pepper
- 2 teaspoons Worcestershire sauce
- ½ teaspoon garlic powder
- ¼ teaspoon red pepper flakes
- ¼ cup chopped parsley

Directions:

1. Preheat the air fryer to 390°F.
2. In a large bowl, place the steak cubes and toss with the salt, pepper, Worcestershire sauce, garlic powder, and red pepper flakes.
3. Pour the steak into the air fryer basket and cook for 10 to 14 minutes, depending on how well done you prefer your bites. Starting at the 8-minute mark, toss the steak bites every 2 minutes to check for doneness.
4. When the steak is cooked, remove it from the basket to a serving bowl and top with the chopped parsley. Allow the steak to rest for 5 minutes before serving.

Creamy Horseradish Roast Beef

Servings: 6
Cooking Time: 65 Minutes + Chilling Time

Ingredients:

- 1 topside roast, tied
- Salt to taste
- 1 tsp butter, melted
- 2 tbsp Dijon mustard
- 3 tbsp prepared horseradish
- 1 garlic clove, minced
- 2/3 cup buttermilk
- 2 tsp red wine
- 1 tbsp minced chives
- Salt and pepper to taste

Directions:

1. Preheat air fryer to 320°F. Mix salt, butter, half of the mustard, 1 tsp of horseradish, and garlic until blended. Rub all over the roast. Bake the roast in the air fryer for 30-35 minutes, flipping once until browned. Transfer to a cutting board and cover with foil. Let rest for 15 minutes.
2. In a bowl, mix buttermilk, horseradish, remaining mustard, chives, wine, salt, and pepper until smooth. Refrigerate. When ready to serve, carve the roast into thin slices and serve with horseradish cream on the side.

Better-than-chinese-take-out Pork Ribs

Servings: 3
Cooking Time: 35 Minutes

Ingredients:

- 1½ tablespoons Hoisin sauce (see here; gluten-free, if a concern)
- 1½ tablespoons Regular or low-sodium soy sauce or gluten-free tamari sauce
- 1½ tablespoons Shaoxing (Chinese cooking rice wine), dry sherry, or white grape juice
- 1½ teaspoons Minced garlic
- ¾ teaspoon Ground dried ginger
- ¾ teaspoon Ground white pepper
- 1½ pounds Pork baby back rib rack(s), cut into 2-bone pieces

Directions:

1. Mix the hoisin sauce, soy or tamari sauce, Shaoxing or its substitute, garlic, ginger, and white pepper in a large bowl. Add the rib sections and stir well to coat. Cover and refrigerate for at least 2 hours or up to 24 hours, stirring the rib sections in the marinade occasionally.
2. Preheat the air fryer to 350°F . Set the ribs in their bowl on the counter as the machine heats.
3. When the machine is at temperature, set the rib pieces on their sides in a single layer in the basket with as much air space between them as possible. Air-fry for 35 minutes, turning and rearranging the pieces once, until deeply browned and sizzling.
4. Use kitchen tongs to transfer the rib pieces to a large serving bowl or platter. Wait a minute or two before serving them so the meat can reabsorb some of its own juices.

Citrus Pork Lettuce Wraps

Servings:4
Cooking Time: 35 Minutes

Ingredients:

- Salt and white pepper to taste
- 1 tbsp cornstarch
- 1 tbsp red wine vinegar
- 2 tbsp orange marmalade
- 1 tsp pulp-free orange juice
- 2 tsp olive oil
- ¼ tsp chili pepper
- ¼ tsp ground ginger
- 1 lb pork loin, cubed
- 8 iceberg lettuce leaves

Directions:

1. Create a slurry by whisking cornstarch and 1 tbsp of water in a bowl. Set aside. Place a small saucepan over medium heat. Add the red wine vinegar, orange marmalade, orange juice, olive oil, chili pepper, and ginger and cook for 3 minutes, stirring continuously. Mix in the slurry and simmer for 1 more minute. Turn the heat off and let it thicken, about3 minutes.
2. Preheat air fryer to 350ºF. Sprinkle the pork with salt and white pepper. Place them in the greased frying basket and Air Fry for 8-10 minutes until cooked through and browned, turning once. Transfer pork cubes to a bowl with the sauce and toss to coat. Serve in lettuce leaves.

Pork & Beef Egg Rolls

Servings: 8
Cooking Time: 8 Minutes

Ingredients:

- ¼ pound very lean ground beef
- ¼ pound lean ground pork
- 1 tablespoon soy sauce
- 1 teaspoon olive oil
- ½ cup grated carrots
- 2 green onions, chopped
- 2 cups grated Napa cabbage
- ¼ cup chopped water chestnuts
- ¼ teaspoon salt
- ¼ teaspoon garlic powder
- ¼ teaspoon black pepper
- 1 egg
- 1 tablespoon water
- 8 egg roll wraps
- oil for misting or cooking spray

Directions:

1. In a large skillet, brown beef and pork with soy sauce. Remove cooked meat from skillet, drain, and set aside.
2. Pour off any excess grease from skillet. Add olive oil, carrots, and onions. Sauté until barely tender, about 1 minute.
3. Stir in cabbage, cover, and cook for 1 minute or just until cabbage slightly wilts. Remove from heat.
4. In a large bowl, combine the cooked meats and vegetables, water chestnuts, salt, garlic powder, and pepper. Stir well. If needed, add more salt to taste.
5. Beat together egg and water in a small bowl.
6. Fill egg roll wrappers, using about ¼ cup of filling for each wrap. Roll up and brush all over with egg wash to seal. Spray very lightly with olive oil or cooking spray.
7. Place 4 egg rolls in air fryer basket and cook at 390°F for 4minutes. Turn over and cook 4 more minutes, until golden brown and crispy.
8. Repeat to cook remaining egg rolls.

POULTRY RECIPES

Chicken Skewers

Servings: 4
Cooking Time: 55 Minutes

Ingredients:

- 1 lb boneless skinless chicken thighs, cut into pieces
- 1 sweet onion, cut into 1-inch pieces
- 1 zucchini, cut into 1-inch pieces
- 1 red bell pepper, cut into 1-inch pieces
- ¼ cup olive oil
- 1 tsp garlic powder
- 1 tsp shallot powder
- 1 tsp ground cumin
- ½ tsp dried oregano
- ½ tsp dried thyme
- ¼ cup lemon juice
- 1 tbsp apple cider vinegar
- 12 grape tomatoes

Directions:

1. Combine the olive oil, garlic powder, shallot powder, cumin, oregano, thyme, lemon juice, and vinegar in a bowl; mix well. Alternate skewering the chicken, bell pepper, onion, zucchini, and tomatoes. Once all of the skewers are prepared, place them in a greased baking dish and pour the olive oil marinade over the top. Turn to coat. Cover with plastic wrap and refrigerate.
2. Preheat air fryer to 380°F. Remove the skewers from the marinade and arrange them in a single layer on the frying basket. Bake for 25 minutes, rotating once. Let the skewers sit for 5 minutes. Serve and enjoy!

Glazed Chicken Thighs

Servings: 4
Cooking Time: 25 Minutes

Ingredients:

- 1 lb boneless, skinless chicken thighs
- ¼ cup balsamic vinegar
- 3 tbsp honey
- 2 tbsp brown sugar
- 1 tsp whole-grain mustard
- ¼ cup soy sauce
- 3 garlic cloves, minced
- Salt and pepper to taste
- ½ tsp smoked paprika
- 2 tbsp chopped shallots

Directions:

1. Preheat air fryer to 375°F. Whisk vinegar, honey, sugar, soy sauce, mustard, garlic, salt, pepper, and paprika in a small bowl. Arrange the chicken in the frying basket and brush the top of each with some of the vinegar mixture. Air Fry for 7 minutes, then flip the chicken. Brush the tops with the rest of the vinegar mixture and Air Fry for another 5 to 8 minutes. Allow resting for 5 minutes before slicing. Serve warm sprinkled with shallots.

Turkey Steaks With Green Salad

Servings: 4
Cooking Time: 20 Minutes

Ingredients:

- 1/3 cup shaved Parmesan cheese
- 3 tsp grated Parmesan cheese
- 4 turkey breast steaks
- Salt and pepper to taste
- 1 large egg, beaten
- ½ cup bread crumbs
- ½ tsp dried thyme
- 5 oz baby spinach
- 5 oz watercress
- 1 tbsp olive oil
- 1 tbsp lemon juice
- 2 spring onions, chopped
- 1 lemon, cut into wedges

Directions:

1. Place the steaks between two sheets of parchment paper. Pound the turkey to ¼-inch thick cutlets using a meat mallet or rolling pin. Season the cutlets with salt and pepper to taste. Put the beaten egg in a shallow bowl. Put the crumbs, thyme, and Parmesan in a second shallow bowl. Dip the cutlet in the egg bowl and then in the crumb mix. Press the crumbs so that they stick to the chicken. Preheat air fryer to 400°F. Fry the turkey in the greased frying basket for 8 minutes, flipping once until golden and cooked through. Repeat for all cutlets.
2. Put the spinach, spring onions, and watercress in a bowl. Toss with olive oil, lemon juice, salt, and pepper. Serve each cutlet on a plate topped with 1 ½ cups salad. Garnish with lemon wedges and shaved Parmesan cheese. Serve.

Pulled Turkey Quesadillas

Servings: 4
Cooking Time: 15 Minutes

Ingredients:

- ¾ cup pulled cooked turkey breast
- 6 tortilla wraps
- 1/3 cup grated Swiss cheese
- 1 small red onion, sliced
- 2 tbsp Mexican chili sauce

Directions:

1. Preheat air fryer to 400°F. Lay 3 tortilla wraps on a clean workspace, then spoon equal amounts of Swiss cheese, turkey, Mexican chili sauce, and red onion on the tortillas. Spritz the exterior of the tortillas with cooking spray. Air Fry the quesadillas, one at a time, for 5-8 minutes. The cheese should be melted and the outsides crispy. Serve.

Chicken Flatbread Pizza With Spinach

Servings: 1
Cooking Time: 15 Minutes

Ingredients:

- ½ cup cooked chicken breast, cubed
- ¼ cup grated mozzarella
- 1 whole-wheat pita
- 1 tbsp olive oil
- 1 garlic clove, minced
- ¼ tsp red pepper flakes
- ½ cup kale
- ¼ sliced red onion

Directions:

1. Preheat air fryer to 380°F.Lightly brush the top of the pita with olive oil and top with the garlic, red pepper flakes, kale, onion, chicken, and mozzarella. Put the pizza into the frying basket and Bake for 7 minutes. Serve.

Chicken Breast Burgers

Servings: 4
Cooking Time: 35 Minutes

Ingredients:

- 2 chicken breasts
- 1 cup dill pickle juice
- 1 cup buttermilk
- 1 egg
- ½ cup flour
- Salt and pepper to taste
- 4 buns
- 2 pickles, sliced

Directions:

1. Cut the chicken into cutlets by cutting them in half horizontally on a cutting board. Transfer them to a large bowl along with pickle juice and ½ cup of buttermilk. Toss to coat, then marinate for 30 minutes in the fridge.
2. Preheat air fryer to 370°F. In a shallow bowl, beat the egg and the rest of the buttermilk to combine. In another shallow bowl, mix flour, salt, and pepper. Dip the marinated cutlet in the egg mixture, then dredge in flour. Place the cutlets in the greased frying basket and Air Fry for 12 minutes, flipping once halfway through. Remove the cutlets and pickles on buns and serve.

Guajillo Chile Chicken Meatballs

Servings:4
Cooking Time: 30 Minutes

Ingredients:

- 1 lb ground chicken
- 1 large egg
- ½ cup bread crumbs
- 1 tbsp sour cream
- 2 tsp brown mustard
- 2 tbsp grated onion
- 2 tbsp tomato paste
- 1 tsp ground cumin
- 1 tsp guajillo chile powder
- 2 tbsp olive oil

Directions:

1. Preheat air fryer to 350°F. Mix the ground chicken, egg, bread crumbs, sour cream, mustard, onion, tomato paste, cumin, and chili powder in a bowl. Form into 16 meatballs. Place the meatballs in the greased frying basket and Air Fry for 8-10 minutes, shaking once until browned and cooked through. Serve immediately.

Sweet-and-sour Chicken

Servings: 6
Cooking Time: 10 Minutes

Ingredients:

- 1 cup pineapple juice
- 1 cup plus 3 tablespoons cornstarch, divided
- ¼ cup sugar
- ¼ cup ketchup
- ¼ cup apple cider vinegar
- 2 tablespoons soy sauce or tamari
- 1 teaspoon garlic powder, divided
- ¼ cup flour
- 1 tablespoon sesame seeds
- ½ teaspoon salt
- ¼ teaspoon ground black pepper
- 2 large eggs
- 2 pounds chicken breasts, cut into 1-inch cubes
- 1 red bell pepper, cut into 1-inch pieces
- 1 carrot, sliced into ¼-inch-thick rounds

Directions:

1. In a medium saucepan, whisk together the pineapple juice, 3 tablespoons of the cornstarch, the sugar, the ketchup, the apple cider vinegar, the soy sauce or tamari, and ½ teaspoon of the garlic powder. Cook over medium-low heat, whisking occasionally as the sauce thickens, about 6 minutes. Stir and set aside while preparing the chicken.
2. Preheat the air fryer to 370°F.
3. In a medium bowl, place the remaining 1 cup of cornstarch, the flour, the sesame seeds, the salt, the remaining ½ teaspoon of garlic powder, and the pepper.
4. In a second medium bowl, whisk the eggs.
5. Working in batches, place the cubed chicken in the cornstarch mixture to lightly coat; then dip it into the egg mixture, and return it to the cornstarch mixture. Shake off the excess and place the coated chicken in the air fryer basket. Spray with cooking spray and cook for 5 minutes, shake the basket, and spray with more cooking spray. Cook an additional 3 to 5 minutes, or until completely cooked and golden brown.
6. On the last batch of chicken, add the bell pepper and carrot to the basket and cook with the chicken.
7. Place the cooked chicken and vegetables into a serving bowl and toss with the sweet-and-sour sauce to serve.

Italian Roasted Chicken Thighs

Servings: 6
Cooking Time: 14 Minutes

Ingredients:

- 6 boneless chicken thighs
- ½ teaspoon dried oregano
- ½ teaspoon garlic powder
- ½ teaspoon sea salt
- ½ teaspoon black pepper
- ¼ teaspoon crushed red pepper flakes

Directions:

1. Pat the chicken thighs with paper towel.
2. In a small bowl, mix the oregano, garlic powder, salt, pepper, and crushed red pepper flakes. Rub the spice mixture onto the chicken thighs.
3. Preheat the air fryer to 400°F.
4. Place the chicken thighs in the air fryer basket and spray with cooking spray. Cook for 10 minutes, turn over, and cook another 4 minutes. When cooking completes, the internal temperature should read 165°F.

Satay Chicken Skewers

Servings: 4
Cooking Time: 35 Minutes

Ingredients:

- 2 chicken breasts, cut into strips
- 1 ½ tbsp Thai red curry paste
- ¼ cup peanut butter
- 1 tbsp maple syrup
- 1 tbsp tamari
- 1 tbsp lime juice
- 2 tsp chopped onions
- ¼ tsp minced ginger
- 1 clove garlic, minced
- 1 cup coconut milk
- 1 tsp fish sauce
- 1 tbsp chopped cilantro

Directions:

1. Mix the peanut butter, maple syrup, tamari, lime juice, ¼ tsp of sriracha, onions, ginger, garlic, and 2 tbsp of water in a bowl. Reserve 1 tbsp of the sauce. Set aside. Combine the reserved peanut sauce, fish sauce, coconut milk, Thai red curry paste, cilantro and chicken strips in a bowl and let marinate in the fridge for 15 minutes.
2. Preheat air fryer at 350ºF. Thread chicken strips onto skewers and place them on a kebab rack. Place rack in the frying basket and Air Fry for 12 minutes. Serve with previously prepared peanut sauce on the side.

Indian Chicken Tandoori

Servings: 2
Cooking Time: 35 Minutes

Ingredients:

- 2 chicken breasts, cubed
- ½ cup hung curd
- 1 tsp turmeric powder
- 1 tsp red chili powder
- 1 tsp chaat masala powder
- Pinch of salt

Directions:

1. Preheat air fryer to 350°F. Mix the hung curd, turmeric, red chili powder, chaat masala powder, and salt in a mixing bowl. Stir until the mixture is free of lumps. Coat the chicken with the mixture, cover, and refrigerate for 30 minutes to marinate. Place the marinated chicken chunks in a baking pan and drizzle with the remaining marinade. Bake for 25 minutes until the chicken is juicy and spiced. Serve warm.

Chipotle Chicken Drumsticks

Servings: 4
Cooking Time: 40 Minutes

Ingredients:

- 1 can chipotle chilies packed in adobe sauce
- 2 tbsp grated Mexican cheese
- 6 chicken drumsticks
- 1 egg, beaten
- ½ cup bread crumbs
- 1 tbsp corn flakes
- Salt and pepper to taste

Directions:

1. Preheat air fryer to 350°F. Place the chilies in the sauce in your blender and pulse until a fine paste is formed. Transfer to a bowl and add the beaten egg. Combine thoroughly. Mix the breadcrumbs, Mexican cheese, corn flakes, salt, and pepper in a separate bowl, and set aside.
2. Coat the chicken drumsticks with the crumb mixture, then dip into the bowl with wet ingredients, then dip again into the dry ingredients. Arrange the chicken drumsticks on the greased frying basket in a single flat layer. Air Fry for 14-16 minutes, turning each chicken drumstick over once. Serve warm.

Prosciutto Chicken Rolls

Servings: 4
Cooking Time: 30 Minutes

Ingredients:

- ½ cup chopped broccoli
- ½ cup grated cheddar
- 2 scallions, sliced
- 2 garlic cloves, minced
- 4 prosciutto thin slices
- ¼ cup cream cheese
- Salt and pepper to taste
- ½ tsp dried oregano
- ½ tsp dried basil
- 4 chicken breasts
- 2 tbsp chopped cilantro

Directions:

1. Preheat air fryer to 375°F. Combine broccoli, scallion, garlic, Cheddar, cream cheese, salt, pepper, oregano, and basil in a small bowl. Prepare the chicken by placing it between two pieces of plastic wrap. Pound the chicken with a meat mallet or heavy can until it is evenly ½-inch thickness. Top each with a slice of prosciutto and spoon ¼ of the cheese mixture in the center of the chicken breast. Fold each breast over the filling and transfer to a greased baking dish. Place the dish in the frying basket and bake for 8 minutes. Flip the chicken and bake for another 8-12 minutes. Allow resting for 5 minutes. Serve warm sprinkled with cilantro and enjoy!

Lemon Herb Whole Cornish Hen

Servings: 2
Cooking Time: 50 Minutes

Ingredients:

- 1 Cornish hen
- ¼ cup olive oil
- 2 tbsp lemon juice
- 2 tbsp sage, chopped
- 2 tbsp thyme, chopped
- 4 garlic cloves, chopped
- Salt and pepper to taste
- 1 celery stalk, chopped
- ½ small onion
- ½ lemon, juiced and zested
- 2 tbsp chopped parsley

Directions:

1. Preheat air fryer to 380°F. Whisk the olive oil, lemon juice, sage, thyme, garlic, salt, and pepper in a bowl. Rub the mixture on the tops and sides of the hen. Pour any excess inside the cavity of the bird. Stuff the celery, onion, and lemon juice and zest into the cavity of the hen. Put in the frying basket and Roast for 40-45 minutes. Cut the hen in half and serve garnished with parsley.

Parmesan Crusted Chicken Cordon Bleu

Servings: 2
Cooking Time: 14 Minutes

Ingredients:

- 2 (6-ounce) boneless, skinless chicken breasts
- salt and freshly ground black pepper
- 1 tablespoon Dijon mustard
- 4 slices Swiss cheese
- 4 slices deli-sliced ham
- ¼ cup all-purpose flour*
- 1 egg, beaten
- ¾ cup panko breadcrumbs*
- ⅓ cup grated Parmesan cheese
- olive oil, in a spray bottle

Directions:

1. Butterfly the chicken breasts. Place the chicken breast on a cutting board and press down on the breast with the palm of your hand. Slice into the long side of the chicken breast, parallel to the cutting board, but not all the way through to the other side. Open the chicken breast like a "book". Place a piece of plastic wrap over the chicken breast and gently pound it with a meat mallet to make it evenly thick.
2. Season the chicken with salt and pepper. Spread the Dijon mustard on the inside of each chicken breast. Layer one slice of cheese on top of the mustard, then top with the 2 slices of ham and the other slice of cheese.
3. Starting with the long edge of the chicken breast, roll the chicken up to the other side. Secure it shut with 1 or 2 toothpicks.
4. Preheat the air fryer to 350°F.
5. Set up a dredging station with three shallow dishes. Place the flour in the first dish. Place the beaten egg in the second shallow dish. Combine the panko breadcrumbs and Parmesan cheese together in the third shallow dish. Dip the stuffed and rolled chicken breasts in the flour, then the beaten egg and then roll in the breadcrumb-cheese mixture to cover on all sides. Press the crumbs onto the chicken breasts with your hands to make sure they are well adhered. Spray the chicken breasts with olive oil and transfer to the air fryer basket.
6. Air-fry at 350°F for 14 minutes, flipping the breasts over halfway through the cooking time. Let the chicken rest for a few minutes before removing the toothpicks, slicing and serving.

Yogurt-marinated Chicken Legs

Servings: 4
Cooking Time: 50 Minutes

Ingredients:

- 1 cup Greek yogurt
- 1 tbsp Dijon mustard
- 1 tsp smoked paprika
- 1 tbsp crushed red pepper
- 1 tsp garlic powder
- 1 tsp dried oregano
- 1 tsp dried thyme
- 1 teaspoon ground cumin
- ¼ cup lemon juice
- Salt and pepper to taste
- 1 ½ lb chicken legs
- 3 tbsp butter, melted

Directions:

1. Combine all ingredients, except chicken and butter, in a bowl. Fold in chicken legs and toss until coated. Let sit covered in the fridge for 60 minutes up to overnight.
2. Preheat air fryer at 375ºF. Shake excess marinade from chicken; place them in the greased frying basket and Air Fry for 18 minutes, brush melted butter and flip once. Let chill for 5 minutes before serving.

Sweet Chili Spiced Chicken

Servings: 4
Cooking Time: 43 Minutes

Ingredients:

- Spice Rub:
- 2 tablespoons brown sugar
- 2 tablespoons paprika
- 1 teaspoon dry mustard powder
- 1 teaspoon chili powder
- 2 tablespoons coarse sea salt or kosher salt
- 2 teaspoons coarsely ground black pepper
- 1 tablespoon vegetable oil
- 1 (3½-pound) chicken, cut into 8 pieces

Directions:

1. Prepare the spice rub by combining the brown sugar, paprika, mustard powder, chili powder, salt and pepper. Rub the oil all over the chicken pieces and then rub the spice mix onto the chicken, covering completely. This is done very easily in a zipper sealable bag. You can do this ahead of time and let the chicken marinate in the refrigerator, or just proceed with cooking right away.
2. Preheat the air fryer to 370°F.
3. Air-fry the chicken in two batches. Place the two chicken thighs and two drumsticks into the air fryer basket. Air-fry at 370°F for 10 minutes. Then, gently turn the chicken pieces over and air-fry for another 10 minutes. Remove the chicken pieces and let them rest on a plate while you cook the chicken breasts. Air-fry the chicken breasts, skin side down for 8 minutes. Turn the chicken breasts over and air-fry for another 12 minutes.
4. Lower the temperature of the air fryer to 340°F. Place the first batch of chicken on top of the second batch already in the basket and air-fry for a final 3 minutes.
5. Let the chicken rest for 5 minutes and serve warm with some mashed potatoes and a green salad or vegetables.

Japanese-inspired Glazed Chicken

Servings: 4
Cooking Time: 25 Minutes

Ingredients:

- 4 chicken breasts
- Chicken seasoning to taste
- Salt and pepper to taste
- 2 tsp grated fresh ginger
- 2 garlic cloves, minced
- ¼ cup molasses
- 2 tbsp tamari sauce

Directions:

1. Preheat air fryer to 400°F. Season the chicken with seasoning, salt, and pepper. Place the chicken in the greased frying basket and Air Fry for 7 minutes, then flip the chicken. Cook for another 3 minutes.
2. While the chicken is cooking, combine ginger, garlic, molasses, and tamari sauce in a saucepan over medium heat. Cook for 4 minutes or until the sauce thickens. Transfer all of the chicken to a serving dish. Drizzle with ginger-tamari glaze and serve.

FISH AND SEAFOOD RECIPES

Corn & Shrimp Boil

Servings: 4
Cooking Time: 40 Minutes

Ingredients:

- 8 frozen "mini" corn on the cob
- 1 tbsp smoked paprika
- 2 tsp dried thyme
- 1 tsp dried marjoram
- 1 tsp sea salt
- 1 tsp garlic powder
- 1 tsp onion powder
- 1 tsp cayenne pepper
- 1 lb baby potatoes, halved
- 1 tbsp olive oil
- 1 lb peeled shrimp, deveined
- 1 avocado, sliced

Directions:

1. Preheat the air fryer to 370°F.Combine the paprika, thyme, marjoram, salt, garlic, onion, and cayenne and mix well. Pour into a small glass jar. Add the potatoes, corn, and olive oil to the frying basket and sprinkle with 2 tsp of the spice mix and toss. Air Fry for 15 minutes, shaking the basket once until tender. Remove and set aside. Put the shrimp in the frying basket and sprinkle with 2 tsp of the spice mix. Air Fry for 5-8 minutes, shaking once until shrimp are tender and pink. Combine all the ingredients in the frying basket and sprinkle with 2 tsp of the spice mix. Toss to coat and cook for 1-2 more minutes or until hot. Serve topped with avocado.

Oyster Shrimp With Fried Rice

Servings: 4
Cooking Time: 40 Minutes

Ingredients:

- 1 lb peeled shrimp, deveined
- 1 shallot, chopped
- 2 garlic cloves, minced
- 1 tbsp olive oil
- 1 tbsp butter
- 2 eggs, beaten
- 2 cups cooked rice
- 1 cup baby peas
- 2 tbsp fish sauce
- 1 tbsp oyster sauce

Directions:

1. Preheat the air fryer to 370°F. Combine the shrimp, shallot, garlic, and olive oil in a cake pan. Put the cake pan in the air fryer and Bake the shrimp for 5-7 minutes, stirring once until shrimp are no pinker. Remove into a bowl, and set aside. Put the butter in the hot cake pan to melt. Add the eggs and return to the fryer. Bake for 4-6 minutes, stirring once until the eggs are set. Remove the eggs from the pan and set aside.
2. Add the rice, peas, oyster sauce, and fish sauce to the pan and return it to the fryer. Bake for 12-15 minutes, stirring once halfway through. Pour in the shrimp and eggs and stir. Cook for 2-3 more minutes until everything is hot.

Chili Blackened Shrimp

Servings: 4
Cooking Time: 15 Minutes

Ingredients:

- 1 lb peeled shrimp, deveined
- 1 tsp paprika
- ½ tsp dried dill
- ½ tsp red chili flakes
- ½ lemon, juiced
- Salt and pepper to taste

Directions:

1. Preheat air fryer to 400°F. In a resealable bag, add shrimp, paprika, dill, red chili flakes, lemon juice, salt and pepper. Seal and shake well. Place the shrimp in the greased frying basket and Air Fry for 7-8 minutes, shaking the basket once until blackened. Let cool slightly and serve.

Beer-breaded Halibut Fish Tacos

Servings: 4
Cooking Time: 10 Minutes

Ingredients:

- 1 pound halibut, cut into 1-inch strips
- 1 cup light beer
- 1 jalapeño, minced and divided
- 1 clove garlic, minced
- ¼ teaspoon ground cumin
- ½ cup cornmeal
- ¼ cup all-purpose flour
- 1¼ teaspoons sea salt, divided
- 2 cups shredded cabbage
- 1 lime, juiced and divided
- ¼ cup Greek yogurt
- ¼ cup mayonnaise
- 1 cup grape tomatoes, quartered
- ½ cup chopped cilantro
- ¼ cup chopped onion
- 1 egg, whisked
- 8 corn tortillas

Directions:

1. In a shallow baking dish, place the fish, the beer, 1 teaspoon of the minced jalapeño, the garlic, and the cumin. Cover and refrigerate for 30 minutes.
2. Meanwhile, in a medium bowl, mix together the cornmeal, flour, and ½ teaspoon of the salt.
3. In large bowl, mix together the shredded cabbage, 1 tablespoon of the lime juice, the Greek yogurt, the mayonnaise, and ½ teaspoon of the salt.
4. In a small bowl, make the pico de gallo by mixing together the tomatoes, cilantro, onion, ¼ teaspoon of the salt, the remaining jalapeño, and the remaining lime juice.
5. Remove the fish from the refrigerator and discard the marinade. Dredge the fish in the whisked egg; then dredge the fish in the cornmeal flour mixture, until all pieces of fish have been breaded.
6. Preheat the air fryer to 350°F.
7. Place the fish in the air fryer basket and spray liberally with cooking spray. Cook for 6 minutes, flip and shake the fish, and cook another 4 minutes.
8. While the fish is cooking, heat the tortillas in a heavy skillet for 1 to 2 minutes over high heat.
9. To assemble the tacos, place the battered fish on the heated tortillas, and top with slaw and pico de gallo. Serve immediately.

Restaurant-style Breaded Shrimp

Servings: 2
Cooking Time: 35 Minutes

Ingredients:

- ½ lb fresh shrimp, peeled
- 2 eggs, beaten
- ½ cup breadcrumbs
- ½ onion, finely chopped
- ½ tsp ground ginger
- ½ tsp garlic powder
- ½ tsp turmeric
- ½ tsp red chili powder
- Salt and pepper to taste
- ½ tsp amchur powder

Directions:

1. Preheat air fryer to 350°F. Place the beaten eggs in a bowl and dip in the shrimp. Blend the bread crumbs with all the dry ingredients in another bowl. Add in the shrimp and toss to coat. Place the coated shrimp in the greased frying basket. Air Fry for 12-14 minutes until the breaded crust of the shrimp is golden brown. Toss the basket two or three times during the cooking time. Serve.

Crab Cakes On A Budget

Servings: 4
Cooking Time: 12 Minutes

Ingredients:

- 8 ounces imitation crabmeat
- 4 ounces leftover cooked fish (such as cod, pollock, or haddock)
- 2 tablespoons minced green onion
- 2 tablespoons minced celery
- ¾ cup crushed saltine cracker crumbs
- 2 tablespoons light mayonnaise
- 1 teaspoon prepared yellow mustard
- 1 tablespoon Worcestershire sauce, plus 2 teaspoons
- 2 teaspoons dried parsley flakes
- ½ teaspoon dried dill weed, crushed
- ½ teaspoon garlic powder
- ½ teaspoon Old Bay Seasoning
- ½ cup panko breadcrumbs
- oil for misting or cooking spray

Directions:

1. Use knives or a food processor to finely shred crabmeat and fish.
2. In a large bowl, combine all ingredients except panko and oil. Stir well.
3. Shape into 8 small, fat patties.
4. Carefully roll patties in panko crumbs to coat. Spray both sides with oil or cooking spray.
5. Place patties in air fryer basket and cook at 390°F for 12 minutes or until golden brown and crispy.

Fish Goujons With Tartar Sauce

Servings: 4
Cooking Time: 20 Minutes

Ingredients:

- ¼ cup flour
- Salt and pepper to taste
- ¼ tsp smoked paprika
- ¼ tsp dried oregano
- 1 tsp dried thyme
- 1 egg
- 4 haddock fillets
- 1 lemon, thinly sliced
- ½ cup tartar sauce

Directions:

1. Preheat air fryer to 400°F. Combine flour, salt, pepper, paprika, thyme, and oregano in a wide bowl. Whisk egg and 1 teaspoon water in another wide bowl. Slice each fillet into 4 strips. Dip the strips in the egg mixture. Then roll them in the flour mixture and coat completely. Arrange the fish strips on the greased frying basket. Air Fry for 4 minutes. Flip the fish and Air Fry for another 4 to 5 minutes until crisp. Serve warm with lemon slices and tartar sauce on the side and enjoy.

Fish Cakes

Servings: 4
Cooking Time: 10 Minutes

Ingredients:

- ¾ cup mashed potatoes (about 1 large russet potato)
- 12 ounces cod or other white fish
- salt and pepper
- oil for misting or cooking spray
- 1 large egg
- ¼ cup potato starch
- ½ cup panko breadcrumbs
- 1 tablespoon fresh chopped chives
- 2 tablespoons minced onion

Directions:

1. Peel potatoes, cut into cubes, and cook on stovetop till soft.
2. Salt and pepper raw fish to taste. Mist with oil or cooking spray, and cook in air fryer at 360°F for 6 to 8minutes, until fish flakes easily. If fish is crowded, rearrange halfway through cooking to ensure all pieces cook evenly.
3. Transfer fish to a plate and break apart to cool.
4. Beat egg in a shallow dish.
5. Place potato starch in another shallow dish, and panko crumbs in a third dish.
6. When potatoes are done, drain in colander and rinse with cold water.
7. In a large bowl, mash the potatoes and stir in the chives and onion. Add salt and pepper to taste, then stir in the fish.
8. If needed, stir in a tablespoon of the beaten egg to help bind the mixture.
9. Shape into 8 small, fat patties. Dust lightly with potato starch, dip in egg, and roll in panko crumbs. Spray both sides with oil or cooking spray.
10. Cook at 360°F for 10 minutes, until golden brown and crispy.

Mediterranean Salmon Cakes

Servings:4
Cooking Time: 30 Minutes

Ingredients:

- ¼ cup heavy cream
- 5 tbsp mayonnaise
- 2 cloves garlic, minced
- ¼ tsp caper juice
- 2 tsp lemon juice
- 1 tbsp capers
- 1 can salmon
- 2 tsp lemon zest
- 1 egg
- ¼ minced red bell peppers
- ½ cup flour
- ⅛ tsp salt
- 2 tbsp sliced green olives

Directions:

1. Combine heavy cream, 2 tbsp of mayonnaise, garlic, caper juices, capers, and lemon juice in a bowl. Place the resulting caper sauce in the fridge until ready to use.
2. Preheat air fryer to 400ºF. Combine canned salmon, lemon zest, egg, remaining mayo, bell peppers, flour, and salt in a bowl. Form into 8 patties. Place the patties in the greased frying basket and Air Fry for 10 minutes, turning once. Let rest for 5 minutes before drizzling with lemon sauce. Garnish with green olives to serve.

Crispy Fish Sandwiches

Servings: 4
Cooking Time: 25 Minutes

Ingredients:

- ½ cup torn iceberg lettuce
- ½ cup mayonnaise
- 1 tbsp Dijon mustard
- ½ cup diced dill pickles
- 1 tsp capers
- 1 tsp tarragon
- 1 tsp dill
- Salt and pepper to taste
- 1/3 cup flour
- 2 tbsp cornstarch
- 1 tsp smoked paprika
- ¼ cup milk
- 1 egg
- ½ cup bread crumbs
- 4 cod fillets, cut in half
- 1 vine-ripe tomato, sliced
- 4 hamburger buns

Directions:

1. Mix the mayonnaise, mustard, pickles, capers, tarragon, dill, salt, and pepper in a small bowl and let the resulting tartare sauce chill covered in the fridge until ready to use. Preheat air fryer at 375ºF. In a bowl, mix the flour, cornstarch, paprika, and salt. In another bowl, beat the milk and egg and in a third bowl, add the breadcrumbs. Roll the cod in the flour mixture, shake off excess flour. Then, dip in the egg, shake off excess egg. Finally, dredge in the breadcrumbs mixture. Place fish pieces in the greased frying basket and Air Fry for 6 minutes, flipping once. Add cooked fish, lettuce, tomato slices, and tartar sauce to each bottom bun and top with the top bun. Serve.

Southern Shrimp With Cocktail Sauce

Servings: 2
Cooking Time: 20 Minutes

Ingredients:

- ½ lb raw shrimp, tail on, deveined and shelled
- 1 cup ketchup
- 2 tbsp prepared horseradish
- 1 tbsp lemon juice
- ½ tsp Worcestershire sauce
- 1/8 tsp chili powder
- Salt and pepper to taste
- 1/3 cup flour
- 2 tbsp cornstarch
- ¼ cup milk
- 1 egg
- ½ cup bread crumbs
- 1 tbsp Cajun seasoning
- 1 lemon, cut into pieces

Directions:

1. In a small bowl, whisk the ketchup, horseradish, lemon juice, Worcestershire sauce, chili powder, salt, and pepper. Let chill covered in the fridge until ready to use. Preheat air fryer at 375ºF. In a bowl, mix the flour, cornstarch, and salt. In another bowl, beat the milk and egg and in a third bowl, combine breadcrumbs and Cajun seasoning.
2. Roll the shrimp in the flour mixture, shake off excess flour. Then, dip in the egg, shake off excess egg. Finally, dredge in the breadcrumbs mixture. Place shrimp in the greased frying basket and Air Fry for 8 minutes, flipping once. Serve with cocktail sauce and lemon slices.

Fish Tortillas With Coleslaw

Servings: 4
Cooking Time: 30 Minutes

Ingredients:

- 1 tbsp olive oil
- 1 lb cod fillets
- 3 tbsp lemon juice
- 2 cups chopped red cabbage
- ½ cup salsa
- 1/3 cup sour cream
- 6 taco shells, warm
- 1 avocado, chopped

Directions:

1. Preheat air fryer to 400°F. Brush oil on the cod and sprinkle with some lemon juice. Place in the frying basket and Air Fry until the fish flakes with a fork, 9-12 minutes.
2. Meanwhile, mix together the remaining lemon juice, red cabbage, salsa, and sour cream in a medium bowl. Put the cooked fish in a bowl, breaking it into large pieces. Then add the cabbage mixture, avocados, and warmed tortilla shells ready for assembly. Enjoy!

British Fish & Chips

Servings: 4
Cooking Time: 40 Minutes

Ingredients:

- 2 peeled russet potatoes, thinly sliced
- 1 egg white
- 1 tbsp lemon juice
- 1/3 cup ground almonds
- 2 bread slices, crumbled
- ½ tsp dried basil
- 4 haddock fillets

Directions:

1. Preheat air fryer to 390°F. Lay the potato slices in the frying basket and Air Fry for 11-15 minutes. Turn the fries a couple of times while cooking. While the fries are cooking, whisk the egg white and lemon juice together in a bowl. On a plate, combine the almonds, breadcrumbs, and basil. First, one at a time, dip the fillets into the egg mix and then coat in the almond/breadcrumb mix. Lay the fillets on a wire rack until the fries are done. Preheat the oven to 350°F. After the fries are done, move them to a pan and place in the oven to keep warm. Put the fish in the frying basket and Air Fry for 10-14 minutes or until cooked through, golden, and crispy. Serve with the fries.

Crab Cakes

Servings: 2
Cooking Time: 10 Minutes

Ingredients:

- 1 teaspoon butter
- ⅓ cup finely diced onion
- ⅓ cup finely diced celery
- ¼ cup mayonnaise
- 1 teaspoon Dijon mustard
- 1 egg
- pinch ground cayenne pepper
- 1 teaspoon salt
- freshly ground black pepper
- 16 ounces lump crabmeat
- ½ cup + 2 tablespoons panko breadcrumbs, divided

Directions:

1. Melt the butter in a skillet over medium heat. Sauté the onion and celery until it starts to soften, but not brown – about 4 minutes. Transfer the cooked vegetables to a large bowl. Add the mayonnaise, Dijon mustard, egg, cayenne pepper, salt and freshly ground black pepper to the bowl. Gently fold in the lump crabmeat and 2 tablespoons of panko breadcrumbs. Stir carefully so you don't break up all the crab pieces.
2. Preheat the air fryer to 400°F.
3. Place the remaining panko breadcrumbs in a shallow dish. Divide the crab mixture into 4 portions and shape each portion into a round patty. Dredge the crab patties in the breadcrumbs, coating both sides as well as the edges with the crumbs.
4. Air-fry the crab cakes for 5 minutes. Using a flat spatula, gently turn the cakes over and air-fry for another 5 minutes. Serve the crab cakes with tartar sauce or cocktail sauce, or dress it up with the suggestion below.

Blackened Red Snapper

Servings: 4
Cooking Time: 8 Minutes

Ingredients:

- 1½ teaspoons black pepper
- ¼ teaspoon thyme
- ¼ teaspoon garlic powder
- ⅛ teaspoon cayenne pepper
- 1 teaspoon olive oil
- 4 4-ounce red snapper fillet portions, skin on
- 4 thin slices lemon
- cooking spray

Directions:

1. Mix the spices and oil together to make a paste. Rub into both sides of the fish.
2. Spray air fryer basket with nonstick cooking spray and lay snapper steaks in basket, skin-side down.
3. Place a lemon slice on each piece of fish.
4. Cook at 390°F for 8 minutes. The fish will not flake when done, but it should be white through the center.

Garlicky Sea Bass With Root Veggies

Servings: 4
Cooking Time: 25 Minutes

Ingredients:

- 1 carrot, diced
- 1 parsnip, diced
- ½ rutabaga, diced
- ½ turnip, diced
- ¼ cup olive oil
- Celery salt to taste
- 4 sea bass fillets
- ½ tsp onion powder
- 2 garlic cloves, minced
- 1 lemon, sliced

Directions:

1. Preheat air fryer to 380°F. Coat the carrot, parsnip, turnip and rutabaga with olive oil and salt in a small bowl. Lightly season the sea bass with and onion powder, then place into the frying basket. Spread the garlic over the top of the fillets, then cover with lemon slices. Pour the prepared vegetables into the basket around and on top of the fish. Roast for 15 minutes. Serve and enjoy!

Maple-crusted Salmon

Servings: 2
Cooking Time: 8 Minutes

Ingredients:

- 12 ounces salmon filets
- ⅓ cup maple syrup
- 1 teaspoon Worcestershire sauce
- 2 teaspoons Dijon mustard or brown mustard
- ½ cup finely chopped walnuts
- ½ teaspoon sea salt
- ½ lemon
- 1 tablespoon chopped parsley, for garnish

Directions:

1. Place the salmon in a shallow baking dish. Top with maple syrup, Worcestershire sauce, and mustard. Refrigerate for 30 minutes.
2. Preheat the air fryer to 350°F.
3. Remove the salmon from the marinade and discard the marinade.
4. Place the chopped nuts on top of the salmon filets, and sprinkle salt on top of the nuts. Place the salmon, skin side down, in the air fryer basket. Cook for 6 to 8 minutes or until the fish flakes in the center.
5. Remove the salmon and plate on a serving platter. Squeeze fresh lemon over the top of the salmon and top with chopped parsley. Serve immediately.

Popcorn Crawfish

Servings: 4
Cooking Time: 18 Minutes

Ingredients:

- ½ cup flour, plus 2 tablespoons
- ½ teaspoon garlic powder
- 1½ teaspoons Old Bay Seasoning
- ½ teaspoon onion powder
- ½ cup beer, plus 2 tablespoons
- 12-ounce package frozen crawfish tail meat, thawed and drained
- oil for misting or cooking spray
- Coating
- 1½ cups panko crumbs
- 1 teaspoon Old Bay Seasoning
- ½ teaspoon ground black pepper

Directions:

1. In a large bowl, mix together the flour, garlic powder, Old Bay Seasoning, and onion powder. Stir in beer to blend.
2. Add crawfish meat to batter and stir to coat.
3. Combine the coating ingredients in food processor and pulse to finely crush the crumbs. Transfer crumbs to shallow dish.
4. Preheat air fryer to 390°F.
5. Pour the crawfish and batter into a colander to drain. Stir with a spoon to drain excess batter.
6. Working with a handful of crawfish at a time, roll in crumbs and place on a cookie sheet. It's okay if some of the smaller pieces of crawfish meat stick together.
7. Spray breaded crawfish with oil or cooking spray and place all at once into air fryer basket.
8. Cook at 390°F for 5minutes. Shake basket or stir and mist again with olive oil or spray. Cook 5 moreminutes, shake basket again, and mist lightly again. Continue cooking 5 more minutes, until browned and crispy.

SANDWICHES AND BURGERS RECIPES

Chicken Gyros

Servings: 4
Cooking Time: 14 Minutes

Ingredients:

- 4 4- to 5-ounce boneless skinless chicken thighs, trimmed of any fat blobs
- 2 tablespoons Lemon juice
- 2 tablespoons Red wine vinegar
- 2 tablespoons Olive oil
- 2 teaspoons Dried oregano
- 2 teaspoons Minced garlic
- 1 teaspoon Table salt
- 1 teaspoon Ground black pepper
- 4 Pita pockets (gluten-free, if a concern)
- ½ cup Chopped tomatoes
- ½ cup Bottled regular, low-fat, or fat-free ranch dressing (gluten-free, if a concern)

Directions:

1. Mix the thighs, lemon juice, vinegar, oil, oregano, garlic, salt, and pepper in a zip-closed bag. Seal, gently massage the marinade into the meat through the plastic, and refrigerate for at least 2 hours or up to 6 hours. (Longer than that and the meat can turn rubbery.)
2. Set the plastic bag out on the counter (to make the contents a little less frigid). Preheat the air fryer to 375°F .
3. When the machine is at temperature, use kitchen tongs to place the thighs in the basket in one layer. Discard the marinade. Air-fry the chicken thighs undisturbed for 12 minutes, or until browned and an instant-read meat thermometer inserted into the thickest part of one thigh registers 165°F. You may need to air-fry the chicken 2 minutes longer if the machine's temperature is 360°F.
4. Use kitchen tongs to transfer the thighs to a cutting board. Cool for 5 minutes, then set one thigh in each of the pita pockets. Top each with 2 tablespoons chopped tomatoes and 2 tablespoons dressing. Serve warm.

Inside Out Cheeseburgers

Servings: 2
Cooking Time: 20 Minutes

Ingredients:

- ¾ pound lean ground beef
- 3 tablespoons minced onion
- 4 teaspoons ketchup
- 2 teaspoons yellow mustard
- salt and freshly ground black pepper
- 4 slices of Cheddar cheese, broken into smaller pieces
- 8 hamburger dill pickle chips

Directions:

1. Combine the ground beef, minced onion, ketchup, mustard, salt and pepper in a large bowl. Mix well to thoroughly combine the ingredients. Divide the meat into four equal portions.
2. To make the stuffed burgers, flatten each portion of meat into a thin patty. Place 4 pickle chips and half of the cheese onto the center of two of the patties, leaving a rim around the edge of the patty exposed. Place the remaining two patties on top of the first and press the meat together firmly, sealing the edges tightly. With the burgers on a flat surface, press the sides of the burger with the palm of your hand to create a straight edge. This will help keep the stuffing inside the burger while it cooks.
3. Preheat the air fryer to 370°F.
4. Place the burgers inside the air fryer basket and air-fry for 20 minutes, flipping the burgers over halfway through the cooking time.
5. Serve the cheeseburgers on buns with lettuce and tomato.

Lamb Burgers

Servings: 3
Cooking Time: 17 Minutes

Ingredients:

- 1 pound 2 ounces Ground lamb
- 3 tablespoons Crumbled feta
- 1 teaspoon Minced garlic
- 1 teaspoon Tomato paste
- ¾ teaspoon Ground coriander
- ¾ teaspoon Ground dried ginger
- Up to ⅛ teaspoon Cayenne
- Up to a ⅛ teaspoon Table salt (optional)
- 3 Kaiser rolls or hamburger buns (gluten-free, if a concern), split open

Directions:

1. Preheat the air fryer to 375°F .
2. Gently mix the ground lamb, feta, garlic, tomato paste, coriander, ginger, cayenne, and salt (if using) in a bowl until well combined, trying to keep the bits of cheese intact. Form this mixture into two 5-inch patties for the small batch, three 5-inch patties for the medium, or four 5-inch patties for the large.
3. Set the patties in the basket in one layer and air-fry undisturbed for 16 minutes, or until an instant-read meat thermometer inserted into one burger registers 160°F. (The cheese is not an issue with the temperature probe in this recipe as it was for the Inside-Out Cheeseburgers, because the feta is so well mixed into the ground meat.)
4. Use a nonstick-safe spatula, and perhaps a flatware fork for balance, to transfer the burgers to a cutting board. Set the buns cut side down in the basket in one layer (working in batches as necessary) and air-fry undisturbed for 1 minute, to toast a bit and warm up. Serve the burgers warm in the buns.

Thanksgiving Turkey Sandwiches

Servings: 3
Cooking Time: 10 Minutes

Ingredients:

- 1½ cups Herb-seasoned stuffing mix (not cornbread-style; gluten-free, if a concern)
- 1 Large egg white(s)
- 2 tablespoons Water
- 3 5- to 6-ounce turkey breast cutlets
- Vegetable oil spray
- 4½ tablespoons Purchased cranberry sauce, preferably whole berry
- ⅛ teaspoon Ground cinnamon
- ⅛ teaspoon Ground dried ginger
- 4½ tablespoons Regular, low-fat, or fat-free mayonnaise (gluten-free, if a concern)
- 6 tablespoons Shredded Brussels sprouts
- 3 Kaiser rolls (gluten-free, if a concern), split open

Directions:

1. Preheat the air fryer to 375°F .
2. Put the stuffing mix in a heavy zip-closed bag, seal it, lay it flat on your counter, and roll a rolling pin over the bag to crush the stuffing mix to the consistency of rough sand. (Or you can pulse the stuffing mix to the desired consistency in a food processor.)
3. Set up and fill two shallow soup plates or small pie plates on your counter: one for the egg white(s), whisked with the water until foamy; and one for the ground stuffing mix.
4. Dip a cutlet in the egg white mixture, coating both sides and letting any excess egg white slip back into the rest. Set the cutlet in the ground stuffing mix and coat it evenly on both sides, pressing gently to coat well on both sides. Lightly coat the cutlet on both sides with vegetable oil spray, set it aside, and continue dipping and coating the remaining cutlets in the same way.
5. Set the cutlets in the basket and air-fry undisturbed for 10 minutes, or until crisp and brown. Use kitchen tongs to transfer the cutlets to a wire rack to cool for a few minutes.
6. Meanwhile, stir the cranberry sauce with the cinnamon and ginger in a small bowl. Mix the shredded Brussels sprouts and mayonnaise in a second bowl until the vegetable is evenly coated.
7. Build the sandwiches by spreading about 1½ tablespoons of the cranberry mixture on the cut side of the bottom half of each roll. Set a cutlet on top, then spread about 3 tablespoons of the Brussels sprouts mixture evenly over the cutlet. Set the other half of the roll on top and serve warm.

Best-ever Roast Beef Sandwiches

Servings: 6
Cooking Time: 30-50 Minutes

Ingredients:

- 2½ teaspoons Olive oil
- 1½ teaspoons Dried oregano
- 1½ teaspoons Dried thyme
- 1½ teaspoons Onion powder
- 1½ teaspoons Table salt
- 1½ teaspoons Ground black pepper
- 3 pounds Beef eye of round
- 6 Round soft rolls, such as Kaiser rolls or hamburger buns (gluten-free, if a concern), split open lengthwise
- ¾ cup Regular, low-fat, or fat-free mayonnaise (gluten-free, if a concern)
- 6 Romaine lettuce leaves, rinsed
- 6 Round tomato slices (¼ inch thick)

Directions:

1. Preheat the air fryer to 350°F .
2. Mix the oil, oregano, thyme, onion powder, salt, and pepper in a small bowl. Spread this mixture all over the eye of round.
3. When the machine is at temperature, set the beef in the basket and air-fry for 30 to 50 minutes (the range depends on the size of the cut), turning the meat twice, until an instant-read meat thermometer inserted into the thickest piece of the meat registers 130°F for rare, 140°F for medium, or 150°F for well-done.
4. Use kitchen tongs to transfer the beef to a cutting board. Cool for 10 minutes. If serving now, carve into ⅛-inch-thick slices. Spread each roll with 2 tablespoons mayonnaise and divide the beef slices between the rolls. Top with a lettuce leaf and a tomato slice and serve. Or set the beef in a container, cover, and refrigerate for up to 3 days to make cold roast beef sandwiches anytime.

Sausage And Pepper Heros

Servings: 3
Cooking Time: 11 Minutes

Ingredients:

- 3 links (about 9 ounces total) Sweet Italian sausages (gluten-free, if a concern)
- 1½ Medium red or green bell pepper(s), stemmed, cored, and cut into ½-inch-wide strips
- 1 medium Yellow or white onion(s), peeled, halved, and sliced into thin half-moons
- 3 Long soft rolls, such as hero, hoagie, or Italian sub rolls (gluten-free, if a concern), split open lengthwise
- For garnishing Balsamic vinegar
- For garnishing Fresh basil leaves

Directions:

1. Preheat the air fryer to 400°F.
2. When the machine is at temperature, set the sausage links in the basket in one layer and air-fry undisturbed for 5 minutes.
3. Add the pepper strips and onions. Continue air-frying, tossing and rearranging everything about once every minute, for 5 minutes, or until the sausages are browned and an instant-read meat thermometer inserted into one of the links registers 160°F.
4. Use a nonstick-safe spatula and kitchen tongs to transfer the sausages and vegetables to a cutting board. Set the rolls cut side down in the basket in one layer (working in batches as necessary) and air-fry undisturbed for 1 minute, to toast the rolls a bit and warm them up. Set 1 sausage with some pepper strips and onions in each warm roll, sprinkle balsamic vinegar over the sandwich fillings, and garnish with basil leaves.

Eggplant Parmesan Subs

Servings: 2
Cooking Time: 13 Minutes

Ingredients:

- 4 Peeled eggplant slices (about ½ inch thick and 3 inches in diameter)
- Olive oil spray
- 2 tablespoons plus 2 teaspoons Jarred pizza sauce, any variety except creamy
- ¼ cup (about ⅔ ounce) Finely grated Parmesan cheese
- 2 Small, long soft rolls, such as hero, hoagie, or Italian sub rolls (gluten-free, if a concern), split open lengthwise

Directions:

1. Preheat the air fryer to 350°F .
2. When the machine is at temperature, coat both sides of the eggplant slices with olive oil spray. Set them in the basket in one layer and air-fry undisturbed for 10 minutes, until lightly browned and softened.
3. Increase the machine's temperature to 375°F (or 370°F, if that's the closest setting—unless the machine is already at 360°F, in which case leave it alone). Top each eggplant slice with 2 teaspoons pizza sauce, then 1 tablespoon cheese. Air-fry undisturbed for 2 minutes, or until the cheese has melted.
4. Use a nonstick-safe spatula, and perhaps a flatware fork for balance, to transfer the eggplant slices cheese side up to a cutting board. Set the roll(s) cut side down in the basket in one layer (working in batches as necessary) and air-fry undisturbed for 1 minute, to toast the rolls a bit and warm them up. Set 2 eggplant slices in each warm roll.

Chicken Apple Brie Melt

Servings: 3
Cooking Time: 13 Minutes

Ingredients:

- 3 5- to 6-ounce boneless skinless chicken breasts
- Vegetable oil spray
- 1½ teaspoons Dried herbes de Provence
- 3 ounces Brie, rind removed, thinly sliced
- 6 Thin cored apple slices
- 3 French rolls (gluten-free, if a concern)
- 2 tablespoons Dijon mustard (gluten-free, if a concern)

Directions:

1. Preheat the air fryer to 375°F .
2. Lightly coat all sides of the chicken breasts with vegetable oil spray. Sprinkle the breasts evenly with the herbes de Provence.
3. When the machine is at temperature, set the breasts in the basket and air-fry undisturbed for 10 minutes.
4. Top the chicken breasts with the apple slices, then the cheese. Air-fry undisturbed for 2 minutes, or until the cheese is melty and bubbling.
5. Use a nonstick-safe spatula and kitchen tongs, for balance, to transfer the breasts to a cutting board. Set the rolls in the basket and air-fry for 1 minute to warm through. (Putting them in the machine without splitting them keeps the insides very soft while the outside gets a little crunchy.)
6. Transfer the rolls to the cutting board. Split them open lengthwise, then spread 1 teaspoon mustard on each cut side. Set a prepared chicken breast on the bottom of a roll and close with its top, repeating as necessary to make additional sandwiches. Serve warm.

Mexican Cheeseburgers

Servings: 4
Cooking Time: 22 Minutes

Ingredients:

- 1¼ pounds ground beef
- ¼ cup finely chopped onion
- ½ cup crushed yellow corn tortilla chips
- 1 (1.25-ounce) packet taco seasoning
- ¼ cup canned diced green chilies
- 1 egg, lightly beaten
- 4 ounces pepper jack cheese, grated
- 4 (12-inch) flour tortillas
- shredded lettuce, sour cream, guacamole, salsa (for topping)

Directions:

1. Combine the ground beef, minced onion, crushed tortilla chips, taco seasoning, green chilies, and egg in a large bowl. Mix thoroughly until combined – your hands are good tools for this. Divide the meat into four equal portions and shape each portion into an oval-shaped burger.
2. Preheat the air fryer to 370°F.
3. Air-fry the burgers for 18 minutes, turning them over halfway through the cooking time. Divide the cheese between the burgers, lower fryer to 340°F and air-fry for an additional 4 minutes to melt the cheese. (This will give you a burger that is medium-well. If you prefer your cheeseburger medium-rare, shorten the cooking time to about 15 minutes and then add the cheese and proceed with the recipe.)
4. While the burgers are cooking, warm the tortillas wrapped in aluminum foil in a 350°F oven, or in a skillet with a little oil over medium-high heat for a couple of minutes. Keep the tortillas warm until the burgers are ready.
5. To assemble the burgers, spread sour cream over three quarters of the tortillas and top each with some shredded lettuce and salsa. Place the Mexican cheeseburgers on the lettuce and top with guacamole. Fold the tortillas around the burger, starting with the bottom and then folding the sides in over the top. (A little sour cream can help hold the seam of the tortilla together.) Serve immediately.

Philly Cheesesteak Sandwiches

Servings: 3
Cooking Time: 9 Minutes

Ingredients:

- ¾ pound Shaved beef
- 1 tablespoon Worcestershire sauce (gluten-free, if a concern)
- ¼ teaspoon Garlic powder
- ¼ teaspoon Mild paprika
- 6 tablespoons (1½ ounces) Frozen bell pepper strips (do not thaw)
- 2 slices, broken into rings Very thin yellow or white medium onion slice(s)
- 6 ounces (6 to 8 slices) Provolone cheese slices
- 3 Long soft rolls such as hero, hoagie, or Italian sub rolls, or hot dog buns (gluten-free, if a concern), split open lengthwise

Directions:

1. Preheat the air fryer to 400°F.
2. When the machine is at temperature, spread the shaved beef in the basket, leaving a ½-inch perimeter around the meat for good air flow. Sprinkle the meat with the Worcestershire sauce, paprika, and garlic powder. Spread the peppers and onions on top of the meat.
3. Air-fry undisturbed for 6 minutes, or until cooked through. Set the cheese on top of the meat. Continue air-frying undisturbed for 3 minutes, or until the cheese has melted.
4. Use kitchen tongs to divide the meat and cheese layers in the basket between the rolls or buns. Serve hot.

Black Bean Veggie Burgers

Servings: 3
Cooking Time: 10 Minutes

Ingredients:

- 1 cup Drained and rinsed canned black beans
- ⅓ cup Pecan pieces
- ⅓ cup Rolled oats (not quick-cooking or steel-cut; gluten-free, if a concern)
- 2 tablespoons (or 1 small egg) Pasteurized egg substitute, such as Egg Beaters (gluten-free, if a concern)
- 2 teaspoons Red ketchup-like chili sauce, such as Heinz
- ¼ teaspoon Ground cumin
- ¼ teaspoon Dried oregano
- ¼ teaspoon Table salt
- ¼ teaspoon Ground black pepper
- Olive oil
- Olive oil spray

Directions:

1. Preheat the air fryer to 400°F.
2. Put the beans, pecans, oats, egg substitute or egg, chili sauce, cumin, oregano, salt, and pepper in a food processor. Cover and process to a coarse paste that will hold its shape like sugar-cookie dough, adding olive oil in 1-teaspoon increments to get the mixture to blend smoothly. The amount of olive oil is actually dependent on the internal moisture content of the beans and the oats. Figure on about 1 tablespoon (three 1-teaspoon additions) for the smaller batch, with proportional increases for the other batches. A little too much olive oil can't hurt, but a dry paste will fall apart as it cooks and a far-too-wet paste will stick to the basket.
3. Scrape down and remove the blade. Using clean, wet hands, form the paste into two 4-inch patties for the small batch, three 4-inch patties for the medium, or four 4-inch patties for the large batch, setting them one by one on a cutting board. Generously coat both sides of the patties with olive oil spray.
4. Set them in the basket in one layer. Air-fry undisturbed for 10 minutes, or until lightly browned and crisp at the edges.
5. Use a nonstick-safe spatula, and perhaps a flatware fork for balance, to transfer the burgers to a wire rack. Cool for 5 minutes before serving.

Thai-style Pork Sliders

Servings: 4
Cooking Time: 15 Minutes

Ingredients:

- 11 ounces Ground pork
- 2½ tablespoons Very thinly sliced scallions, white and green parts
- 4 teaspoons Minced peeled fresh ginger
- 2½ teaspoons Fish sauce (gluten-free, if a concern)
- 2 teaspoons Thai curry paste (see the headnote; gluten-free, if a concern)
- 2 teaspoons Light brown sugar
- ¾ teaspoon Ground black pepper
- 4 Slider buns (gluten-free, if a concern)

Directions:

1. Preheat the air fryer to 375°F .
2. Gently mix the pork, scallions, ginger, fish sauce, curry paste, brown sugar, and black pepper in a bowl until well combined. With clean, wet hands, form about ⅓ cup of the pork mixture into a slider about 2½ inches in diameter. Repeat until you use up all the meat—3 sliders for the small batch, 4 for the medium, and 6 for the large. (Keep wetting your hands to help the patties adhere.)
3. When the machine is at temperature, set the sliders in the basket in one layer. Air-fry undisturbed for 14 minutes, or until the sliders are golden brown and caramelized at their edges and an instant-read meat thermometer inserted into the center of a slider registers 160°F.
4. Use a nonstick-safe spatula, and perhaps a flatware fork for balance, to transfer the sliders to a cutting board. Set the buns cut side down in the basket in one layer (working in batches as necessary) and air-fry undisturbed for 1 minute, to toast a bit and warm up. Serve the sliders warm in the buns.

Crunchy Falafel Balls

Servings: 8
Cooking Time: 16 Minutes

Ingredients:

- 2½ cups Drained and rinsed canned chickpeas
- ¼ cup Olive oil
- 3 tablespoons All-purpose flour
- 1½ teaspoons Dried oregano
- 1½ teaspoons Dried sage leaves
- 1½ teaspoons Dried thyme
- ¾ teaspoon Table salt
- Olive oil spray

Directions:

1. Preheat the air fryer to 400°F.
2. Place the chickpeas, olive oil, flour, oregano, sage, thyme, and salt in a food processor. Cover and process into a paste, stopping the machine at least once to scrape down the inside of the canister.
3. Scrape down and remove the blade. Using clean, wet hands, form 2 tablespoons of the paste into a ball, then continue making 9 more balls for a small batch, 15 more for a medium one, and 19 more for a large batch. Generously coat the balls in olive oil spray.
4. Set the balls in the basket in one layer with a little space between them and air-fry undisturbed for 16 minutes, or until well browned and crisp.
5. Dump the contents of the basket onto a wire rack. Cool for 5 minutes before serving.

Chili Cheese Dogs

Servings: 3
Cooking Time: 12 Minutes

Ingredients:

- ¾ pound Lean ground beef
- 1½ tablespoons Chile powder
- 1 cup plus 2 tablespoons Jarred sofrito
- 3 Hot dogs (gluten-free, if a concern)
- 3 Hot dog buns (gluten-free, if a concern), split open lengthwise
- 3 tablespoons Finely chopped scallion
- 9 tablespoons (a little more than 2 ounces) Shredded Cheddar cheese

Directions:

1. Crumble the ground beef into a medium or large saucepan set over medium heat. Brown well, stirring often to break up the clumps. Add the chile powder and cook for 30 seconds, stirring the whole time. Stir in the sofrito and bring to a simmer. Reduce the heat to low and simmer, stirring occasionally, for 5 minutes. Keep warm.
2. Preheat the air fryer to 400°F.
3. When the machine is at temperature, put the hot dogs in the basket and air-fry undisturbed for 10 minutes, or until the hot dogs are bubbling and blistered, even a little crisp.
4. Use kitchen tongs to put the hot dogs in the buns. Top each with a ½ cup of the ground beef mixture, 1 tablespoon of the minced scallion, and 3 tablespoons of the cheese. (The scallion should go under the cheese so it superheats and wilts a bit.) Set the filled hot dog buns in the basket and air-fry undisturbed for 2 minutes, or until the cheese has melted.
5. Remove the basket from the machine. Cool the chili cheese dogs in the basket for 5 minutes before serving.

Chicken Spiedies

Servings: 3
Cooking Time: 12 Minutes

Ingredients:

- 1¼ pounds Boneless skinless chicken thighs, trimmed of any fat blobs and cut into 2-inch pieces
- 3 tablespoons Red wine vinegar
- 2 tablespoons Olive oil
- 2 tablespoons Minced fresh mint leaves
- 2 tablespoons Minced fresh parsley leaves
- 2 teaspoons Minced fresh dill fronds
- ¾ teaspoon Fennel seeds
- ¾ teaspoon Table salt
- Up to a ¼ teaspoon Red pepper flakes
- 3 Long soft rolls, such as hero, hoagie, or Italian sub rolls (gluten-free, if a concern), split open lengthwise
- 4½ tablespoons Regular or low-fat mayonnaise (not fat-free; gluten-free, if a concern)
- 1½ tablespoons Distilled white vinegar
- 1½ teaspoons Ground black pepper

Directions:

1. Mix the chicken, vinegar, oil, mint, parsley, dill, fennel seeds, salt, and red pepper flakes in a zip-closed plastic bag. Seal, gently massage the marinade ingredients into the meat, and refrigerate for at least 2 hours or up to 6 hours. (Longer than that and the meat can turn rubbery.)
2. Set the plastic bag out on the counter (to make the contents a little less frigid). Preheat the air fryer to 400°F.
3. When the machine is at temperature, use kitchen tongs to set the chicken thighs in the basket (discard any remaining marinade) and air-fry undisturbed for 6 minutes. Turn the thighs over and continue air-frying undisturbed for 6 minutes more, until well browned, cooked through, and even a little crunchy.
4. Dump the contents of the basket onto a wire rack and cool for 2 or 3 minutes. Divide the chicken evenly between the rolls. Whisk the mayonnaise, vinegar, and black pepper in a small bowl until smooth. Drizzle this sauce over the chicken pieces in the rolls.

Dijon Thyme Burgers

Servings: 3
Cooking Time: 18 Minutes

Ingredients:

- 1 pound lean ground beef
- ⅓ cup panko breadcrumbs
- ¼ cup finely chopped onion
- 3 tablespoons Dijon mustard
- 1 tablespoon chopped fresh thyme
- 4 teaspoons Worcestershire sauce
- 1 teaspoon salt
- freshly ground black pepper
- Topping (optional):
- 2 tablespoons Dijon mustard
- 1 tablespoon dark brown sugar
- 1 teaspoon Worcestershire sauce
- 4 ounces sliced Swiss cheese, optional

Directions:

1. Combine all the burger ingredients together in a large bowl and mix well. Divide the meat into 4 equal portions and then form the burgers, being careful not to over-handle the meat. One good way to do this is to throw the meat back and forth from one hand to another, packing the meat each time you catch it. Flatten the balls into patties, making an indentation in the center of each patty with your thumb (this will help it stay flat as it cooks) and flattening the sides of the burgers so that they will fit nicely into the air fryer basket.
2. Preheat the air fryer to 370°F.
3. If you don't have room for all four burgers, air-fry two or three burgers at a time for 8 minutes. Flip the burgers over and air-fry for another 6 minutes.
4. While the burgers are cooking combine the Dijon mustard, dark brown sugar, and Worcestershire sauce in a small bowl and mix well. This optional topping to the burgers really adds a boost of flavor at the end. Spread the Dijon topping evenly on each burger. If you cooked the burgers in batches, return the first batch to the cooker at this time – it's ok to place the fourth burger on top of the others in the center of the basket. Air-fry the burgers for another 3 minutes.
5. Finally, if desired, top each burger with a slice of Swiss cheese. Lower the air fryer temperature to 330°F and air-fry for another minute to melt the cheese. Serve the burgers on toasted brioche buns, dressed the way you like them.

Reuben Sandwiches

Servings: 2
Cooking Time: 11 Minutes

Ingredients:

- ½ pound Sliced deli corned beef
- 4 teaspoons Regular or low-fat mayonnaise (not fat-free)
- 4 Rye bread slices
- 2 tablespoons plus 2 teaspoons Russian dressing
- ½ cup Purchased sauerkraut, squeezed by the handful over the sink to get rid of excess moisture
- 2 ounces (2 to 4 slices) Swiss cheese slices (optional)

Directions:

1. Set the corned beef in the basket, slip the basket into the machine, and heat the air fryer to 400°F. Air-fry undisturbed for 3 minutes from the time the basket is put in the machine, just to warm up the meat.
2. Use kitchen tongs to transfer the corned beef to a cutting board. Spread 1 teaspoon mayonnaise on one side of each slice of rye bread, rubbing the mayonnaise into the bread with a small flatware knife.
3. Place the bread slices mayonnaise side down on a cutting board. Spread the Russian dressing over the "dry" side of each slice. For one sandwich, top one slice of bread with the corned beef, sauerkraut, and cheese (if using). For two sandwiches, top two slices of bread each with half of the corned beef, sauerkraut, and cheese (if using). Close the sandwiches with the remaining bread, setting it mayonnaise side up on top.
4. Set the sandwich(es) in the basket and air-fry undisturbed for 8 minutes, or until browned and crunchy.
5. Use a nonstick-safe spatula, and perhaps a flatware fork for balance, to transfer the sandwich(es) to a cutting board. Cool for 2 or 3 minutes before slicing in half and serving.

Chicken Club Sandwiches

Servings: 3
Cooking Time: 15 Minutes

Ingredients:

- 3 5- to 6-ounce boneless skinless chicken breasts
- 6 Thick-cut bacon strips (gluten-free, if a concern)
- 3 Long soft rolls, such as hero, hoagie, or Italian sub rolls (gluten-free, if a concern)
- 3 tablespoons Regular, low-fat, or fat-free mayonnaise (gluten-free, if a concern)
- 3 Lettuce leaves, preferably romaine or iceberg
- 6 ¼-inch-thick tomato slices

Directions:

1. Preheat the air fryer to 375°F .
2. Wrap each chicken breast with 2 strips of bacon, spiraling the bacon around the meat, slightly overlapping the strips on each revolution. Start the second strip of bacon farther down the breast but on a line with the start of the first strip so they both end at a lined-up point on the chicken breast.
3. When the machine is at temperature, set the wrapped breasts bacon-seam side down in the basket with space between them. Air-fry undisturbed for 12 minutes, until the bacon is browned, crisp, and cooked through and an instant-read meat thermometer inserted into the center of a breast registers 165°F. You may need to add 2 minutes in the air fryer if the temperature is at 360°F.
4. Use kitchen tongs to transfer the breasts to a wire rack. Split the rolls open lengthwise and set them cut side down in the basket. Air-fry for 1 minute, or until warmed through.
5. Use kitchen tongs to transfer the rolls to a cutting board. Spread 1 tablespoon mayonnaise on the cut side of one half of each roll. Top with a chicken breast, lettuce leaf, and tomato slice. Serve warm.

DESSERTS AND SWEETS RECIPES

Apple Dumplings

Servings: 4
Cooking Time: 25 Minutes

Ingredients:

- 1 Basic Pie Dough (see the following recipe)
- 4 medium Granny Smith or Pink Lady apples, peeled and cored
- 4 tablespoons sugar
- 4 teaspoons cinnamon
- ½ teaspoon ground nutmeg
- 4 tablespoons unsalted butter, melted
- 4 scoops ice cream, for serving

Directions:

1. Preheat the air fryer to 330°F.
2. Bring the pie crust recipe to room temperature.
3. Place the pie crust on a floured surface. Divide the dough into 4 equal pieces. Roll out each piece to ¼-inch-thick rounds. Place an apple onto each dough round. Sprinkle 1 tablespoon of sugar in the core part of each apple; sprinkle 1 teaspoon cinnamon and ⅛ teaspoon nutmeg over each. Place 1 tablespoon of butter into the center of each. Fold up the sides and fully cover the cored apples.
4. Place the dumplings into the air fryer basket and spray with cooking spray. Cook for 25 minutes. Check after 14 minutes cooking; if they're getting too brown, reduce the heat to 320°F and complete the cooking.
5. Serve hot apple dumplings with a scoop of ice cream.

Orange-chocolate Cake

Servings: 6
Cooking Time: 35 Minutes

Ingredients:

- ¾ cup flour
- ½ cup sugar
- 7 tbsp cocoa powder
- ½ tsp baking soda
- ½ cup milk
- 2 ½ tbsp sunflower oil
- ½ tbsp orange juice
- 2 tsp vanilla
- 2 tsp orange zest
- 3 tbsp butter, softened
- 1 ¼ cups powdered sugar

Directions:

1. Use a whisk to combine the flour, sugar, 2 tbsp of cocoa powder, baking soda, and a pinch of salt in a bowl. Once combined, add milk, sunflower oil, orange juice, and orange zest. Stir until combined. Preheat the air fryer to 350°F. Pour the batter into a greased cake pan and Bake for 25 minutes or until a knife inserted in the center comes out clean.
2. Use an electric beater to beat the butter and powdered sugar together in a bowl. Add the remaining cocoa powder and vanilla and whip until fluffy. Scrape the sides occasionally. Refrigerate until ready to use. Allow the cake to cool completely, then run a knife around the edges of the baking pan. Turn it upside-down on a plate so it can be frosted on the sides and top. When the frosting is no longer cold, use a butter knife or small spatula to frost the sides and top. Cut into slices and enjoy!

Mango Cobbler With Raspberries

Servings: 4
Cooking Time: 30 Minutes

Ingredients:

- 1 ½ cups chopped mango
- 1 cup raspberries
- 1 tbsp brown sugar
- 2 tsp cornstarch
- 1 tsp lemon juice
- 2 tbsp sunflower oil
- 1 tbsp maple syrup
- 1 tsp vanilla
- ½ cup rolled oats
- 1/3 cup flour
- 3 tbsp coconut sugar
- 1 tsp cinnamon
- ¼ tsp nutmeg
- ⅛ tsp salt

Directions:

1. Place the mango, raspberries, brown sugar, cornstarch, and lemon juice in a baking pan. Stir with a rubber spatula until combined. Set aside.
2. In a separate bowl, add the oil, maple syrup, and vanilla and stir well. Toss in the oats, flour, coconut sugar, cinnamon, nutmeg, and salt. Stir until combined. Sprinkle evenly over the mango-raspberry filling. Preheat air fryer to 320°F. Bake for 20 minutes or until the topping is crispy and golden. Enjoy warm.

Baked Stuffed Pears

Servings: 4
Cooking Time: 15 Minutes + Cooling Time

Ingredients:

- 4 cored pears, halved
- ½ cup chopped cashews
- ½ cup dried cranberries
- ¼ cup agave nectar
- ½ stick butter, softened
- ½ tsp ground cinnamon
- ½ cup apple juice

Directions:

1. Preheat the air fryer to 350°F. Combine the cashews, cranberries, agave nectar, butter, and cinnamon and mix well. Stuff this mixture into the pears, heaping it up on top. Set the pears in a baking pan and pour the apple juice into the bottom of the pan. Put the pan in the fryer and Bake for 10-12 minutes or until the pears are tender. Let cool before serving.

Nutella Torte

Servings: 6
Cooking Time: 55 Minutes

Ingredients:

- ¼ cup unsalted butter, softened
- ½ cup sugar
- 2 eggs
- 1 teaspoon vanilla
- 1¼ cups Nutella® (or other chocolate hazelnut spread), divided
- ¼ cup flour
- 1 teaspoon baking powder
- ¼ teaspoon salt
- dark chocolate fudge topping
- coarsely chopped toasted hazelnuts

Directions:

1. Cream the butter and sugar together with an electric hand mixer until light and fluffy. Add the eggs, vanilla, and ¾ cup of the Nutella® and mix until combined. Combine the flour, baking powder and salt together, and add these dry ingredients to the butter mixture, beating for 1 minute.
2. Preheat the air fryer to 350°F.
3. Grease a 7-inch cake pan with butter and then line the bottom of the pan with a circle of parchment paper. Grease the parchment paper circle as well. Pour the batter into the prepared cake pan and wrap the pan completely with aluminum foil. Lower the pan into the air fryer basket with an aluminum sling (fold a piece of aluminum foil into a strip about 2-inches wide by 24-inches long). Fold the ends of the aluminum foil over the top of the dish before returning the basket to the air fryer. Air-fry for 30 minutes. Remove the foil and air-fry for another 25 minutes.
4. Remove the cake from air fryer and let it cool for 10 minutes. Invert the cake onto a plate, remove the parchment paper and invert the cake back onto a serving platter. While the cake is still warm, spread the remaining ½ cup of Nutella® over the top of the cake. Melt the dark chocolate fudge in the microwave for about 10 seconds so it melts enough to be pourable. Drizzle the sauce on top of the cake in a zigzag motion. Turn the cake 90 degrees and drizzle more sauce in zigzags perpendicular to the first zigzags. Garnish the edges of the torte with the toasted hazelnuts and serve.

Ricotta Stuffed Apples

Servings: 4
Cooking Time: 25 Minutes

Ingredients:

- ½ cup cheddar cheese
- ¼ cup raisins
- 2 apples
- ½ tsp ground cinnamon

Directions:

1. Preheat air fryer to 350°F. Combine cheddar cheese and raisins in a bowl and set aside. Chop apples lengthwise and discard the core and stem. Sprinkle each half with cinnamon and stuff each half with 1/4 of the cheddar mixture. Bake for 7 minutes, turn, and Bake for 13 minutes more until the apples are soft. Serve immediately.

Banana Bread Cake

Servings: 6
Cooking Time: 18-22 Minutes

Ingredients:

- ¾ cup plus 2 tablespoons All-purpose flour
- ½ teaspoon Baking powder
- ¼ teaspoon Baking soda
- ¼ teaspoon Table salt
- 4 tablespoons (¼ cup/½ stick) Butter, at room temperature
- ½ cup Granulated white sugar
- 2 Small ripe bananas, peeled
- 5 tablespoons Pasteurized egg substitute, such as Egg Beaters
- ¼ cup Buttermilk
- ¾ teaspoon Vanilla extract
- Baking spray (see here)

Directions:

1. Preheat the air fryer to 325°F (or 330°F, if that's the closest setting).
2. Mix the flour, baking powder, baking soda, and salt in a small bowl until well combined.
3. Using an electric hand mixer at medium speed, beat the butter and sugar in a medium bowl until creamy and smooth, about 3 minutes, occasionally scraping down the inside of the bowl.
4. Beat in the bananas until smooth. Then beat in egg substitute or egg, buttermilk, and vanilla until uniform. (The batter may look curdled at this stage. The flour mixture will smooth it out.) Add the flour mixture and beat at low speed until smooth and creamy.
5. Use the baking spray to generously coat the inside of a 6-inch round cake pan for a small batch, a 7-inch round cake pan for a medium batch, or an 8-inch round cake pan for a large batch. Scrape and spread the batter into the pan, smoothing the batter out to an even layer.
6. Set the pan in the basket and air-fry for 18 minutes for a 6-inch layer, 20 minutes for a 7-inch layer, or 22 minutes for an 8-inch layer, or until the cake is well browned and set even if there's a little soft give right at the center. Start checking it at the 16-minute mark to know where you are.
7. Use hot pads or silicone baking mitts to transfer the cake pan to a wire rack. To unmold, set a cutting board over the baking pan and invert both the board and the pan. Lift the still-warm pan off the cake layer. Set the wire rack on top of that layer and invert all of it with the cutting board so that the cake layer is now right side up on the wire rack. Remove the cutting board and continue cooling the cake for at least 10 minutes or to room temperature, about 40 minutes, before slicing into wedges.

Apple-carrot Cupcakes

Servings: 6
Cooking Time: 25 Minutes

Ingredients:

- 1 cup grated carrot
- 1/3 cup chopped apple
- ¼ cup raisins
- 2 tbsp maple syrup
- 1/3 cup milk
- 1 cup oat flour
- 1 tsp ground cinnamon
- ½ tsp ground ginger
- 1 tsp baking powder
- ½ tsp baking soda
- 1/3 cup chopped walnuts

Directions:

1. Preheat air fryer to 350°F. Combine carrot, apple, raisins, maple syrup, and milk in a bowl. Stir in oat flour, cinnamon, ginger, baking powder, and baking soda until combined. Divide the batter between 6 cupcake molds. Top with chopped walnuts each and press down a little. Bake for 15 minutes until golden brown and a toothpick comes out clean. Let cool completely before serving.

Annie's Chocolate Chunk Hazelnut Cookies

Servings: 24
Cooking Time: 12 Minutes

Ingredients:

- 1 cup butter, softened
- 1 cup brown sugar
- ½ cup granulated sugar
- 2 eggs, lightly beaten
- 1½ teaspoons vanilla extract
- 1½ cups all-purpose flour
- ½ cup rolled oats
- 1 teaspoon baking soda
- ½ teaspoon salt
- 2 cups chocolate chunks
- ½ cup toasted chopped hazelnuts

Directions:

1. Cream the butter and sugars together until light and fluffy using a stand mixer or electric hand mixer. Add the eggs and vanilla, and beat until well combined.
2. Combine the flour, rolled oats, baking soda and salt in a second bowl. Gradually add the dry ingredients to the wet ingredients with a wooden spoon or spatula. Stir in the chocolate chunks and hazelnuts until distributed throughout the dough.
3. Shape the cookies into small balls about the size of golf balls and place them on a baking sheet. Freeze the cookie balls for at least 30 minutes, or package them in as airtight a package as you can and keep them in your freezer.
4. When you're ready for a delicious snack or dessert, Preheat the air fryer to 350°F. Cut a piece of parchment paper to fit the number of cookies you are baking. Place the parchment down in the air fryer basket and place the frozen cookie ball or balls on top (remember to leave room for them to expand).
5. Air-fry the cookies at 350°F for 12 minutes, or until they are done to your liking. Let them cool for a few minutes before enjoying your freshly baked cookie.

Boston Cream Donut Holes

Servings: 24
Cooking Time: 12 Minutes

Ingredients:

- 1½ cups bread flour
- 1 teaspoon active dry yeast
- 1 tablespoon sugar
- ¼ teaspoon salt
- ½ cup warm milk
- ½ teaspoon pure vanilla extract
- 2 egg yolks
- 2 tablespoons butter, melted
- vegetable oil
- Custard Filling:
- 1 (3.4-ounce) box French vanilla instant pudding mix
- ¾ cup whole milk
- ¼ cup heavy cream
- Chocolate Glaze:
- 1 cup chocolate chips
- ⅓ cup heavy cream

Directions:

1. Combine the flour, yeast, sugar and salt in the bowl of a stand mixer. Add the milk, vanilla, egg yolks and butter. Mix until the dough starts to come together in a ball. Transfer the dough to a floured surface and knead the dough by hand for 2 minutes. Shape the dough into a ball, place it in a large oiled bowl, cover the bowl with a clean kitchen towel and let the dough rise for 1 to 1½ hours or until the dough has doubled in size.
2. When the dough has risen, punch it down and roll it into a 24-inch log. Cut the dough into 24 pieces and roll each piece into a ball. Place the dough balls on a baking sheet and let them rise for another 30 minutes.
3. Preheat the air fryer to 400°F.
4. Spray or brush the dough balls lightly with vegetable oil and air-fry eight at a time for 4 minutes, turning them over halfway through the cooking time.
5. While donut holes are cooking, make the filling and chocolate glaze. To make the filling, use an electric hand mixer to beat the French vanilla pudding, milk and ¼ cup of heavy cream together for 2 minutes.
6. To make the chocolate glaze, place the chocolate chips in a medium-sized bowl. Bring the heavy cream to a boil on the stovetop and pour it over the chocolate chips. Stir until the chips are melted and the glaze is smooth.
7. To fill the donut holes, place the custard filling in a pastry bag with a long tip. Poke a hole into the side of the donut hole with a small knife. Wiggle the knife around to make room for the filling. Place the pastry bag tip into the hole and slowly squeeze the custard into the center of the donut. Dip the top half of the donut into the chocolate glaze, letting any excess glaze drip back into the bowl. Let the glazed donut holes sit for a few minutes before serving.

Berry Streusel Cake

Servings: 6
Cooking Time: 60 Minutes

Ingredients:

- 2 tbsp demerara sugar
- 2 tbsp sunflower oil
- ¼ cup almond flour
- 1 cup pastry flour
- ½ cup brown sugar
- 1 tsp baking powder
- 1 tbsp lemon zest
- ¼ tsp salt
- ¾ cup milk
- 2 tbsp olive oil
- 1 tsp vanilla
- 1 cup blueberries
- ½ cup powdered sugar
- 1 tbsp lemon juice
- ⅛ tsp salt

Directions:

1. Mix the demerara sugar, sunflower oil, and almond flour in a bowl and put it in the refrigerator. Whisk the pastry flour, brown sugar, baking powder, lemon zest, and salt in another bowl. Add the milk, olive oil, and vanilla and stir with a rubber spatula until combined. Add the blueberries and stir slowly. Coat the inside of a baking pan with oil and pour the batter into the pan.
2. Preheat air fryer to 310°F. Remove the almond mix from the fridge and spread it over the cake batter. Put the cake in the air fryer and Bake for 45 minutes or until a knife inserted in the center comes out clean and the top is golden. Combine the powdered sugar, lemon juice and salt in a bowl. Once the cake has cooled, slice it into 4 pieces and drizzle each with icing. Serve.

Honey-roasted Mixed Nuts

Servings: 8
Cooking Time: 15 Minutes

Ingredients:

- ½ cup raw, shelled pistachios
- ½ cup raw almonds
- 1 cup raw walnuts
- 2 tablespoons filtered water
- 2 tablespoons honey
- 1 tablespoon vegetable oil
- 2 tablespoons sugar
- ½ teaspoon salt

Directions:

1. Preheat the air fryer to 300°F.
2. Lightly spray an air-fryer-safe pan with olive oil; then place the pistachios, almonds, and walnuts inside the pan and place the pan inside the air fryer basket.
3. Cook for 15 minutes, shaking the basket every 5 minutes to rotate the nuts.
4. While the nuts are roasting, boil the water in a small pan and stir in the honey and oil. Continue to stir while cooking until the water begins to evaporate and a thick sauce is formed. Note: The sauce should stick to the back of a wooden spoon when mixed. Turn off the heat.
5. Remove the nuts from the air fryer (cooking should have just completed) and spoon the nuts into the stovetop pan. Use a spatula to coat the nuts with the honey syrup.
6. Line a baking sheet with parchment paper and spoon the nuts onto the sheet. Lightly sprinkle the sugar and salt over the nuts and let cool in the refrigerator for at least 2 hours.
7. When the honey and sugar have hardened, store the nuts in an airtight container in the refrigerator.

Strawberry Pastry Rolls

Servings: 4
Cooking Time: 6 Minutes

Ingredients:

- 3 ounces low-fat cream cheese
- 2 tablespoons plain yogurt
- 2 teaspoons sugar
- ¼ teaspoon pure vanilla extract
- 8 ounces fresh strawberries
- 8 sheets phyllo dough
- butter-flavored cooking spray
- ¼–½ cup dark chocolate chips (optional)

Directions:

1. In a medium bowl, combine the cream cheese, yogurt, sugar, and vanilla. Beat with hand mixer at high speed until smooth, about 1 minute.
2. Wash strawberries and destem. Chop enough of them to measure ½ cup. Stir into cheese mixture.
3. Preheat air fryer to 330°F.
4. Phyllo dough dries out quickly, so cover your stack of phyllo sheets with waxed paper and then place a damp dish towel on top of that. Remove only one sheet at a time as you work.
5. To create one pastry roll, lay out a single sheet of phyllo. Spray lightly with butter-flavored spray, top with a second sheet of phyllo, and spray the second sheet lightly.
6. Place a quarter of the filling (about 3 tablespoons) about ½ inch from the edge of one short side. Fold the end of the phyllo over the filling and keep rolling a turn or two. Fold in both the left and right sides so that the edges meet in the middle of your roll. Then roll up completely. Spray outside of pastry roll with butter spray.
7. When you have 4 rolls, place them in the air fryer basket, seam side down, leaving some space in between each. Cook at 330°F for 6 minutes, until they turn a delicate golden brown.
8. Repeat step 7 for remaining rolls.
9. Allow pastries to cool to room temperature.
10. When ready to serve, slice the remaining strawberries. If desired, melt the chocolate chips in microwave or double boiler. Place 1 pastry on each dessert plate, and top with sliced strawberries. Drizzle melted chocolate over strawberries and onto plate.

Fried Snickers Bars

Servings:8
Cooking Time: 4 Minutes

Ingredients:

- ⅓ cup All-purpose flour
- 1 Large egg white(s), beaten until foamy
- 1½ cups (6 ounces) Vanilla wafer cookie crumbs
- 8 Fun-size (0.6-ounce/17-gram) Snickers bars, frozen
- Vegetable oil spray

Directions:

1. Preheat the air fryer to 400°F.
2. Set up and fill three shallow soup plates or small pie plates on your counter: one for the flour, one for the beaten egg white(s), and one for the cookie crumbs.
3. Unwrap the frozen candy bars. Dip one in the flour, turning it to coat on all sides. Gently shake off any excess, then set it in the beaten egg white(s). Turn it to coat all sides, even the ends, then let any excess egg white slip back into the rest. Set the candy bar in the cookie crumbs. Turn to coat on all sides, even the ends. Dip the candy bar back in the egg white(s) a second time, then into the cookie crumbs a second time, making sure you have an even coating all around. Coat the covered candy bar all over with vegetable oil spray. Set aside so you can dip and coat the remaining candy bars.
4. Set the coated candy bars in the basket with as much air space between them as possible. Air-fry undisturbed for 4 minutes, or until golden brown.
5. Remove the basket from the machine and let the candy bars cool in the basket for 10 minutes. Use a non-stick-safe spatula to transfer them to a wire rack and cool for 5 minutes more before chowing down.

Caramel Apple Crumble

Servings: 6
Cooking Time: 50 Minutes

Ingredients:

- 4 apples, peeled and thinly sliced
- 2 tablespoons sugar
- 1 tablespoon flour
- 1 teaspoon ground cinnamon
- ¼ teaspoon ground allspice
- healthy pinch ground nutmeg
- 10 caramel squares, cut into small pieces
- Crumble Topping:
- ¾ cup rolled oats
- ¼ cup sugar
- ⅓ cup flour
- ¼ teaspoon ground cinnamon
- 6 tablespoons butter, melted

Directions:

1. Preheat the air fryer to 330°F.
2. Combine the apples, sugar, flour, and spices in a large bowl and toss to coat. Add the caramel pieces and mix well. Pour the apple mixture into a 1-quart round baking dish that will fit in your air fryer basket (6-inch diameter).
3. To make the crumble topping, combine the rolled oats, sugar, flour and cinnamon in a small bowl. Add the melted butter and mix well. Top the apples with the crumble mixture. Cover the entire dish with aluminum foil and transfer the dish to the air fryer basket, lowering the dish into the basket using a sling made of aluminum foil (fold a piece of aluminum foil into a strip about 2-inches wide by 24-inches long). Fold the ends of the aluminum foil over the top of the dish before returning the basket to the air fryer.
4. Air-fry at 330°F for 25 minutes. Remove the aluminum foil and continue to air-fry for another 25 minutes. Serve the crumble warm with whipped cream or vanilla ice cream, if desired.

Black And Blue Clafoutis

Servings: 2
Cooking Time: 15minutes

Ingredients:

- 6-inch pie pan
- 3 large eggs
- ½ cup sugar
- 1 teaspoon vanilla extract
- 2 tablespoons butter, melted 1 cup milk
- ½ cup all-purpose flour*
- 1 cup blackberries
- 1 cup blueberries
- 2 tablespoons confectioners' sugar

Directions:

1. Preheat the air fryer to 320°F.
2. Combine the eggs and sugar in a bowl and whisk vigorously until smooth, lighter in color and well combined. Add the vanilla extract, butter and milk and whisk together well. Add the flour and whisk just until no lumps or streaks of white remain.
3. Scatter half the blueberries and blackberries in a greased (6-inch) pie pan or cake pan. Pour half of the batter (about 1¼ cups) on top of the berries and transfer the tart pan to the air fryer basket. You can use an aluminum foil sling to help with this by taking a long piece of aluminum foil, folding it in half lengthwise twice until it is roughly 26-inches by 3-inches. Place this under the pie dish and hold the ends of the foil to move the pie dish in and out of the air fryer basket. Tuck the ends of the foil beside the pie dish while it cooks in the air fryer.
4. Air-fry at 320°F for 15 minutes or until the clafoutis has puffed up and is still a little jiggly in the center. Remove the clafoutis from the air fryer, invert it onto a plate and let it cool while you bake the second batch. Serve the clafoutis warm, dusted with confectioners' sugar on top.

Tortilla Fried Pies

Servings: 12
Cooking Time: 5 Minutes

Ingredients:

- 12 small flour tortillas (4-inch diameter)
- ½ cup fig preserves
- ¼ cup sliced almonds
- 2 tablespoons shredded, unsweetened coconut
- oil for misting or cooking spray

Directions:

1. Wrap refrigerated tortillas in damp paper towels and heat in microwave 30 seconds to warm.
2. Working with one tortilla at a time, place 2 teaspoons fig preserves, 1 teaspoon sliced almonds, and ½ teaspoon coconut in the center of each.
3. Moisten outer edges of tortilla all around.
4. Fold one side of tortilla over filling to make a half-moon shape and press down lightly on center. Using the tines of a fork, press down firmly on edges of tortilla to seal in filling.
5. Mist both sides with oil or cooking spray.
6. Place hand pies in air fryer basket close but not overlapping. It's fine to lean some against the sides and corners of the basket. You may need to cook in 2 batches.
7. Cook at 390°F for 5minutes or until lightly browned. Serve hot.
8. Refrigerate any leftover pies in a closed container. To serve later, toss them back in the air fryer basket and cook for 2 or 3minutes to reheat.

Honey-pecan Yogurt Cake

Servings: 6
Cooking Time: 18-24 Minutes

Ingredients:

- 1 cup plus 3½ tablespoons All-purpose flour
- ¼ teaspoon Baking powder
- ¼ teaspoon Baking soda
- ¼ teaspoon Table salt
- 5 tablespoons Plain full-fat, low-fat, or fat-free Greek yogurt
- 5 tablespoons Honey
- 5 tablespoons Pasteurized egg substitute, such as Egg Beaters
- 2 teaspoons Vanilla extract
- ⅔ cup Chopped pecans
- Baking spray (see here)

Directions:

1. Preheat the air fryer to 325°F (or 330°F, if the closest setting).
2. Mix the flour, baking powder, baking soda, and salt in a small bowl until well combined.
3. Using an electric hand mixer at medium speed , beat the yogurt, honey, egg substitute or egg, and vanilla in a medium bowl until smooth, about 2 minutes, scraping down the inside of the bowl once or twice.
4. Turn off the mixer; scrape down and remove the beaters. Fold in the flour mixture with a rubber spatula, just until all of the flour has been moistened. Fold in the pecans until they are evenly distributed in the mixture.
5. Use the baking spray to generously coat the inside of a 6-inch round cake pan for a small batch, a 7-inch round cake pan for a medium batch, or an 8-inch round cake pan for a large batch. Scrape and spread the batter into the pan, smoothing the batter out to an even layer.
6. Set the pan in the basket and air-fry for 18 minutes for a 6-inch layer, 22 minutes for a 7-inch layer, or 24 minutes for an 8-inch layer, or until a toothpick or cake tester inserted into the center of the cake comes out clean. Start checking it at the 15-minute mark to know where you are.
7. Use hot pads or silicone baking mitts to transfer the cake pan to a wire rack. Cool for 5 minutes. To unmold, set a cutting board over the baking pan and invert both the board and the pan. Lift the still-warm pan off the cake layer. Set the wire rack on top of that layer and invert all of it with the cutting board so that the cake layer is now right side up on the wire rack. Remove the cutting board and continue cooling the cake for at least 10 minutes or to room temperature, about 30 minutes, before slicing into wedges.

APPENDIX A: Measurement Conversions

BASIC KITCHEN CONVERSIONS & EQUIVALENTS

DRY MEASUREMENTS CONVERSION CHART

3 TEASPOONS = 1 TABLESPOON = 1/16 CUP

6 TEASPOONS = 2 TABLESPOONS = 1/8 CUP

12 TEASPOONS = 4 TABLESPOONS = 1/4 CUP

24 TEASPOONS = 8 TABLESPOONS = 1/2 CUP

36 TEASPOONS = 12 TABLESPOONS = 3/4 CUP

48 TEASPOONS = 16 TABLESPOONS = 1 CUP

METRIC TO US COOKING CONVERSIONS

OVEN TEMPERATURES

120 °C = 250 °F

160 °C = 320 °F

180° C = 350 °F

205 °C = 400 °F

220 °C = 425 °F

LIQUID MEASUREMENTS CONVERSION CHART

8 FLUID OUNCES = 1 CUP = 1/2 PINT = 1/4 QUART

16 FLUID OUNCES = 2 CUPS = 1 PINT = 1/2 QUART

32 FLUID OUNCES = 4 CUPS = 2 PINTS = 1 QUART

= 1/4 GALLON

128 FLUID OUNCES = 16 CUPS = 8 PINTS = 4 QUARTS = 1 GALLON

BAKING IN GRAMS

1 CUP FLOUR = 140 GRAMS

1 CUP SUGAR = 150 GRAMS

1 CUP POWDERED SUGAR = 160 GRAMS

1 CUP HEAVY CREAM = 235 GRAMS

VOLUME

1 MILLILITER = 1/5 TEASPOON

5 ML = 1 TEASPOON

15 ML = 1 TABLESPOON

240 ML = 1 CUP OR 8 FLUID OUNCES

1 LITER = 34 FL. OUNCES

WEIGHT

1 GRAM = .035 OUNCES

100 GRAMS = 3.5 OUNCES

500 GRAMS = 1.1 POUNDS

1 KILOGRAM = 35 OUNCES

US TO METRIC COOKING CONVERSIONS

1/5 TSP = 1 ML

1 TSP = 5 ML

1 TBSP = 15 ML

1 FL OUNCE = 30 ML

1 CUP = 237 ML

1 PINT (2 CUPS) = 473 ML

1 QUART (4 CUPS) = .95 LITER

1 GALLON (16 CUPS) = 3.8 LITERS

1 OZ = 28 GRAMS

1 POUND = 454 GRAMS

BUTTER

1 CUP BUTTER = 2 STICKS = 8 OUNCES = 230 GRAMS = 8 TABLESPOONS

WHAT DOES 1 CUP EQUAL

1 CUP = 8 FLUID OUNCES

1 CUP = 16 TABLESPOONS

1 CUP = 48 TEASPOONS

1 CUP = 1/2 PINT

1 CUP = 1/4 QUART

1 CUP = 1/16 GALLON

1 CUP = 240 ML

BAKING PAN CONVERSIONS

1 CUP ALL-PURPOSE FLOUR = 4.5 OZ

1 CUP ROLLED OATS = 3 OZ 1 LARGE EGG = 1.7 OZ

1 CUP BUTTER = 8 OZ 1 CUP MILK = 8 OZ

1 CUP HEAVY CREAM = 8.4 OZ

1 CUP GRANULATED SUGAR = 7.1 OZ

1 CUP PACKED BROWN SUGAR = 7.75 OZ

1 CUP VEGETABLE OIL = 7.7 OZ

1 CUP UNSIFTED POWDERED SUGAR = 4.4 OZ

BAKING PAN CONVERSIONS

9-INCH ROUND CAKE PAN = 12 CUPS

10-INCH TUBE PAN =16 CUPS

11-INCH BUNDT PAN = 12 CUPS

9-INCH SPRINGFORM PAN = 10 CUPS

9 X 5 INCH LOAF PAN = 8 CUPS

9-INCH SQUARE PAN = 8 CUPS

Appendix B : Recipes Index

Printed in Great Britain
by Amazon

36692572R00059